MICHELLE
KWAN
Figure Skater

Todd Peterson

Ferguson
An imprint of Infobase Publishing

Michelle Kwan: Figure Skater

Ferguson
An imprint of Infobase Publishing
132 West 31st Street
New York NY 10001

Library of Congress Cataloging-in-Publication Data

Peterson, Todd (Todd D.), 1969–
  Michelle Kwan : figure skater / Todd Peterson.
      p. cm.
  Includes index.
  ISBN 0-8160-6104-1 (hc : alk. paper)
  1. Kwan, Michelle, 1980—Juvenile literature. 2. Skaters—United States—Biography—Juvenile literature. 3. Women skaters—United States—Biography—Juvenile literature. I. Title.
  GV850.K93P48 2006
  796.91'2'092—dc22   2005011833

Ferguson books are available at special discounts when purchased in bulk quantities for businesses, associations, institutions, or sales promotions. Please call our Special Sales Department in New York at (212) 967-8800 or (800) 322-8755.

You can find Ferguson on the World Wide Web at http://www.fergpubco.com

Text design by David Strelecky

Pages 98–111 adapted from Ferguson's *Encyclopedia of Careers and Vocational Guidance, Thirteenth Edition*

Printed in the United States of America

MP JT 10 9 8 7 6 5 4 3 2 1

This book is printed on acid-free paper.

CONTENTS

1

SKATING TO EXCELLENCE

Like flying. That was how women's figure skating champion Michelle Kwan would recall her stunning performances at the 1998 U.S. National Championships in Philadelphia. For those who witnessed Kwan's short and long programs, words were not enough to describe the perfect balance of artistry and athleticism delivered by the 17-year-old skater. Her flawless execution stunned not only the crowd, but also many of the judges—a group not easily amazed—who rewarded her with scores the likes of which had never before been seen in figure skating.

But the drama that ended that night in Philadelphia actually began a couple of weeks earlier when it had seemed as if Kwan might not even compete in Nationals. Michelle was recovering from a stress fracture in her left foot that she sustained during Skate Canada in Halifax, Nova Scotia, a couple of months before. Kwan had managed to capture first place in the event over her rival, Tara Lipinski, much as she had done at Skate America in Detroit a few weeks earlier. But at the competition in Canada, Kwan felt a sharp pain in her foot that was severe enough to send her to the doctor. There, tests revealed the stress fracture in the second toe—an injury that required a cast for her foot and some time away from the ice.

This fracture could not have come at a worse point in her young career. Michelle had spent most of 1997 trying to recapture what she felt was most important about skating: her love of the sport. The 1996–97 season had been a devastating one for Kwan, a time in which she had relinquished both her national and world titles to the 14-year-old Lipinski, just one year after becoming the youngest American ever to capture the World Championship. Instead of enjoying her success, Kwan was consumed with the idea of winning. "It was as if I was caught up in my own web," she said. "I kept asking myself, 'Why am I here if I don't love it? Why am I torturing myself?' It's supposed to be fun, and I thought I'd die if I didn't win."

Michelle's victories at Skate America and Skate Canada seemed to prove that she was back where she belonged. As far as she was concerned, the fracture was an injury she did not deserve. Michelle asked her coach, Frank Carroll, why this was happening to her.

Michelle gives a stunning performance at the 1998 U.S.
National Championships in Philadelphia. (Associated Press)

The fracture required Kwan to wear a cast for nearly two weeks. The original injury to her toe had occurred months earlier, but it was the grueling workouts in the weeks leading up to Nationals that aggravated the fracture. The pain became so bad that Michelle could hardly walk, let alone skate.

When she finally did return to the rink, she had already missed the Champions Series Final in Munich in mid-December. At first, her practice sessions proved to be as much an exercise in pain as they were a return to form. Michelle could not complete many of her jumps, and those that she did execute often caused her to wince in pain. Around Christmas, with Nationals just two weeks away, Michelle wondered whether she would be able to compete at all.

But she knew that she could not let this opportunity pass. The 1998 Olympic Games in Nagano, Japan, were just around the corner, followed by the World Championships. If she bowed out of Nationals, there was no guarantee that she would earn a spot on the Olympic team. Back on the ice, Kwan was altering her program, reorganizing jumps that she would have launched with her injured left foot. Still, she could not complete a triple flip—a necessary part of her program that required three revolutions in the air—during practice.

Then, the 1998 National Championships were about to begin and Michelle was in Philadelphia in front of thousands of cheering skating fans. And something remarkable happened.

Short but Unforgettable

Recovering from her injury and eager to return to the ice, Kwan was missing a crucial element of her short program: the music. In addition to the routine itself, there are many factors that make up a successful program, for instance, music, costume, and cosmetics. Music might be the most significant of all, as a skater not only has to integrate her program with the music, but she also has to interpret the music as well.

In preparation for the '98 Nationals, Michelle had listened to numerous CDs, searching for the perfect arrangement that would capture the essence of her program. It was Lori Nichol, Michelle's longtime choreographer, who brought Kwan a piece by Russian-born composer Sergei Rachmaninoff, considered by many to be one of the greatest pianists of his time.

January 7, 1998, the night before Kwan's short program and her return to the rink, was a fitful night for the young skater. She lay awake, wondering about her performance and her injury. When she finally did fall asleep, she overslept and missed her morning practice, something that almost never happened. Michelle was too disciplined an athlete to just not show up. It seemed an ominous beginning to her comeback. But then, before she knew it, Michelle was on the ice with the somber, swelling strains of Rachmaninoff's *Finale* providing the perfect accompaniment to a program that was about to shatter all records.

At two-and-a-half-minutes in length, figure skating's short program, often referred to as the technical program, requires skaters to complete eight elements that are then judged on their technical merit. It is, in a manner of speaking, the nuts and bolts of a skater's routine, and it is used to determine where that skater performs in the event's long program. This is critical, because due to the scoring system set up for figure skating, skaters who perform later in the event have a better chance of scoring higher. Those who perform near the beginning of the long program, no matter how well they skate, must be scored lower to allow the skaters who follow them room to improve on that score. Therefore, a skater who leads the long program and executes a flawless routine might only receive a score of 5.8, because there is a chance that someone later in the lineup might perform even better, and every judge has to allow for that.

A score of 0 is given to someone who does not compete, and beyond that scores range from 1, for a bad performance, to 6, for a perfect score. Both of those extremes are incredibly rare. In between are scores of 2 (a poor performance), 3 (average), 4 (a good performance), and 5 (excellent). Additional rankings subdivided in the tenths are then added and subtracted to the scores, so that skaters receive final numbers such as 4.9 and 5.3. Among the top-tier skaters, scores in the excellent range (5.0 and above) are not uncommon.

What was uncommon, however, were the scores that the nine judges turned over when Kwan completed her short program: 5.9, 6.0, 6.0, 6.0, 6.0, 6.0, 5.9, 6.0, 6.0. Michelle had received seven perfect scores from her judges. Many judges *never* award a 6.0—and two of those who gave Kwan her perfect score had never given a 6.0 prior to her performance. In fact, no woman had ever earned a 6.0 from any judge for the National Championships' short program before Michelle's performance. Only one male skater had ever earned more perfect scores in the event: Brian Boitano, Michelle's inspiration, who earned eight 6.0 scores at the 1988 Nationals.

After completing her program and seeing her scores, Michelle summed up her performance in one word: "Wow!"

The Long Program

Kwan's short program had so stunned some fans that many assumed her over-the-top performance was a fluke.

Many thought that with the long program, Michelle would skate an excellent program—and probably even win the competition—but not at the level at which she skated the short program.

Unlike the rather last-minute choice of Rachmaninoff's *Finale*, Michelle's music for the long program had been selected well in advance. *Lyra Angelica*, written in the 1950s by British composer William Alwyn, was a light, sprightly piece that seemingly transported Kwan off the ice, out of the competition, and into a world all her own. "When I hear that music, it always reminds me of angels and clouds," Michelle told one reporter after the program. "That's what I think of while skating. That I'm free, and I'm going to cloud nine."

The long program, also known as the "free skate" or "artistic program," is the four-minute exercise (four-and-a-half minutes for men) in which a skater is able to demonstrate her artistic side.

For Kwan, these few minutes served to illustrate an elegance that had never before been seen in the long program. To begin, she hit a triple-Lutz, double-toe loop combination—a series of moves that requires the skater to take off from one foot and land on the other (the Lutz), followed by a jump that originates from a back outside edge of a skate and finishes on the same edge (loop jump). When the toe pick is used to propel the skater skyward, it is called a toe loop.

Michelle followed her impressive first combination with another back-to-back move, a triple loop–double loop maneuver, and four more triple jumps as well. Near the close of her program, she later said that she asked herself what she would have to do in order to win the competition. She finished with a move that was not part of her repertoire: an improvised triple toe loop.

In front of nearly 20,000 fans, some waving placards declaring their love for her, Michelle was ethereal in her light-blue velvet dress. She later said that seeing those signs and those expressions from her fans made her want "to melt right there on the ice." When her scores for the long program were revealed, the judges ranked it even higher than her short program, with eight perfect 6.0s and one 5.9 score.

"I was crying during her long program," choreographer Lori Nichol later said. "The people around me were crying, too. That's what you hope to do with a program. They were enraptured by what Michelle was doing on the ice."

At least one observer noted that the young skater had "redefined the horizons of her sport," but for Kwan, it was only the beginning. After she saw the perfect scores the judges had awarded her, she started thinking, "What can I do to improve this?"

With 15 of 18 perfect scores in the competition—a record unlikely to be paralleled anytime soon—and the 1998 Winter Olympics in Nagano, Japan, less than a month away, Michelle Kwan had the world at her feet.

2

BEGINNING ON THE ICE

Michelle Kwan has often said that it is impossible to talk about herself, or her success, without first discussing her family. Indeed, the Kwan family's support and dedication to Michelle, as well as her siblings, is a driving force behind her triumphs. In a sport so demanding and consuming as figure skating, it is unlikely that either Michelle or her sister, Karen, who also spent many years as a competitive figure skater, would have achieved so much had it not been for their parents' sacrifices.

Building a New Life

Michelle's father first came to the United States in 1971. A native of China, Danny Kwan relocated to southern California at the age of 22, after visiting the States for a wedding. Danny, born in a small Chinese village but raised in Hong Kong, was taken with life in the United

States, and he saw in this country a place where he could create the kind of life he wanted for himself.

It was not easy. Kwan worked a series of jobs, starting at a restaurant where he first learned how to cook. From there, Danny was hired at a telephone company in Los Angeles—a job he would maintain for many years—but soon he and a partner branched out to open a restaurant on the side: The Golden Pheasant. Located in Torrance,

Michelle and her father, Danny Kwan. Michelle's parents have always been very supportive of her figure skating career. (Corbis)

California, south of Los Angeles, Danny Kwan pushed himself to succeed in this new business venture.

It was a few years later, when he was back in Hong Kong for a school reunion, that Danny became reunited with Estella, Michelle's mother. Danny and Estella had actually spent part of their childhood together, attending the same school. Estella had been born in Hong Kong, and when Danny's family relocated there, the children's families became friends while the two youngsters went to the same school.

Recounting her parents' meeting, Michelle writes in her 1997 autobiography, *Heart of a Champion*, that Danny always had a secret crush on Estella, but that the two did not have much in common. Estella was one of the top students in her class, while Danny, who had not attended school until his family's move to Hong Kong, had a lot of catching up to do with regard to his studies.

Later, after Danny had moved to the United States, Estella pursued a couple of careers, first as a nurse and later as a television news anchorwoman. She was working as an anchorwoman when Danny returned for the reunion and, after becoming reacquainted, the two fell in love and were soon married. In 1975 the new couple returned to the United States, where Danny, Estella, and Danny's parents settled in Torrance, near the Golden Pheasant. The next year Ron, Michelle's brother, was born, followed in 1978 by the birth of Karen, Michelle's older sister. According to Michelle, her parents had decided to stop with two children. "They didn't want to see any of their kids suffering because there wasn't enough to go around," she writes in her autobiography.

"Little Kwan" Comes Along

But things do not always turn out as expected, and in 1979 Estella discovered she was pregnant again. Michelle Kwan, named for one of her father's favorite songs by the British rock group the Beatles, was born on July 7, 1980, in Torrance.

As the youngest member of the family Michelle quickly earned the nickname "Little Kwan." By all accounts, her early life was like that of many children growing up in the United States. She was close with her brother and sister, but both eventually went to school first before Michelle was old enough to do so.

She and Karen briefly took gymnastics lessons, but Michelle has said she does not remember much about her life before she began skating. That may be due to the fact that she first took to the ice when she was just five years old.

It was her brother, Ron, who provided the inspiration for both Michelle and Karen to begin skating. Ron had started to play ice hockey, and soon his sisters began following their older brother to the rink. Michelle wanted to skate from the start, but her parents balked at the idea because she was so young. But even then she demonstrated some of the headstrong will and determination that would later serve her so well in competition. "I cried that it wasn't fair that I was being left out of the fun just because I was only five years old," Michelle remembers. Soon, her parents relented, and Michelle and Karen were both on the ice.

From the moment that Michelle took to skating, she had little time for anything else. She and Karen skated at an ice rink in a mall not far from the family's house. At first, they started taking group lessons, where they learned the most important trick in skating: how to fall. Michelle thought it amusing that they should have to learn that, but later she realized how crucial it is to fall properly so that you do not hurt yourself.

The lessons were basic, beginner information, and Michelle soon hungered for more. She and Karen quickly picked up on the sport, and before long it was suggested that the girls might want to take private lessons that would afford them one-on-one instruction. For Michelle, the individual lessons could not have come fast enough. "Ever since my first lesson, I've always been impatient to learn more," she wrote in her autobiography. "I'm always saying, 'Okay, I've got it. What's next?' I still feel that way."

Soon Michelle was mastering the basics, learning how to push forward with one foot (which is called stroking) and sail along on the ice (known as gliding). Before long she was practicing moves such as the waltz jump, in which the skater steps forward onto an outside edge of her blade and leaps into a half-turn in the air. Other rudimentary moves followed, and because of her small size Michelle was soon sailing through the air.

A Brief History of Figure Skating

Although figure skating originated in Europe, America has had a long fascination with the sport and has greatly shaped the competitions as they are held today. Figure skating originally was a rigid, prim sport. In the 19th century, skaters were stiff, their maneuvers executed with sharp, angular movements. The flowing, artistic skating of an athlete like Michelle Kwan would not have been permitted in many places.

Around the middle part of the 1800s, just before the Civil War, America was caught up in a skating and dancing craze. A New Yorker by the name of Jackson Haines combined the two interests, developing a new style of skating that was similar to dancing on ice. However, much of the country was not ready for this type of performance. Audiences greeted Haines's new style coolly, which led him to leave the United States and head to Europe.

There, he was warmly welcomed in Vienna, where his pioneering method was developed into what would become known as the "international style of figure skating." Still, it would take several decades—not until the early 1900s—before Americans would embrace this style. In 1921 the United States Figure Skating Association, which has since been shortened to U.S. Figure Skating, was born. Membership in the organization allows skaters and their clubs to compete in international events such as the Olympics and the World Championships.

A skater's skills are determined by tests that are sanctioned by U.S. Figure Skating. There are eight levels in the women's singles skating category, beginning with pre-preliminary (the lowest level) and concluding with senior ladies (the highest). Most young skaters spend a year at each level, learning the various spins and jumps, as they slowly climb the competition ladder. Not Michelle Kwan.

Sister Act

Michelle was not alone in her pursuit of skating greatness. From the beginning, Michelle and her sister, Karen, were the best of friends. On the ice, Danny and Estella urged their daughters to work hard, but also to have fun and be themselves. The Kwans also vowed that they would do whatever was necessary to see their girls succeed, so long as Michelle and Karen gave it their all.

Although Michelle admits she is a very competitive person, she says she never felt any competition between her and Karen. Part of that, says Michelle, was because they were so different. For one thing, Karen (who came to be known as "Big Kwan") was a good deal bigger than Michelle (she would eventually grow to be six inches taller than Michelle). This difference in size would ultimately lead to very different skating styles. And even though they tried dressing alike early on, Michelle soon realized that she would have to develop her own style in clothing. Regardless, the two of them were inseparable. "We were together on the ice, off the ice, in the morning, in the evening," writes Michelle in her autobiography.

Together, then, they started their climb up the figure skating ladder. Both sisters started to become better skaters. They were learning all they could from the private lessons at the local rink. By the time the 1988 Winter Games rolled around, Michelle had taken to wearing her skating costume to school, where she would imagine her next lesson. But it was Brian Boitano's gold-medal victory that set the young skater's thoughts reeling. "I tried to imagine what he was feeling," Kwan wrote in *Heart of a Champion*. "Right then I decided that I wanted to know that feeling for *myself*. I vowed that *I* would go to the Olympics." She started counting forward, envisioning how old she would be when the 1994, '98, '02 Olympic Games

Watching the performances of Olympic figure skater Brian Boitano inspired Michelle to one day make it to the Olympics herself. (Getty Images)

and beyond rolled around. "I told myself that I would be at all those Olympics," says Kwan. "I didn't know that you had to qualify to get in. I thought you could just show up."

As Michelle and Karen mastered everything they could at their local private lessons, Danny Kwan started to search for a more proficient instructor for his daughters. Soon the girls were practicing at a new rink in Torrance four and then five times a week. Some of the practices began so early that Michelle and Karen took to sleeping in their skating tights so that they could jump out of bed and be ready to go. The only problem, says Michelle, was that the tights were incredibly uncomfortable to sleep in.

Eventually the girls started to compete, first locally, and then, as they moved up levels in U.S. Figure Skating, in bigger and more competitive events. But with these increasing competitions came more demands on the entire Kwan family. More events meant more costumes, more training, more time, and more money—a lot of it.

The cost of providing the necessary equipment and training for a young skater has been estimated at $50,000 a year and more for serious competitors. In addition to lessons and costumes, it is costly to rent rink time, buy boots and blades, and pay for travel and living expenses, among other things. Nowadays, Michelle is a world-famous athlete with plenty of money. But that was not always the case.

The Cost of Success

Both of Michelle's parents worked exceptionally hard. Danny continued his job at the phone company, while Estella went on to manage the restaurant. In addition, they had to chauffeur the girls to their events and practices and keep things running smoothly at home. But eventually the costs of meeting Michelle's and Karen's skating needs began to overwhelm the family.

The girls had to stop taking lessons and continue practicing on their own. Hand-me-down clothes were the norm, Michelle remembers, and the family collected its spare change that Estella used to buy groceries and other necessities. Finally, Danny and Estella sold the house that the family lived in and moved in with Michelle's grandparents in Torrance. "It would be a long time before we could afford a place of our own again," she wrote in *Heart of a Champion*.

The sale of the house, Michelle wrote, allowed the Kwans to pay off their bills, but it did not allow them to save much money beyond that. Years later, Danny Kwan affirmed the family's financial situation, noting that his children had to go without many things that other young people had. "We struggled for a long time," he said.

But those sacrifices were paying off for Michelle and Karen. The girls were quickly moving up the ranks in U.S. Figure Skating (then known as the United States

Figure Skating Association), headed for the highest desig-
nation of skater: the senior division.

When Michelle and Karen had first started competing
seriously, Danny had told the girls that the family would
do everything it could to support them, so long as the
girls reached the senior level within five years. It was not
so much that he wanted to push his daughters, he told one
reporter, but that the cost of skating was hard on the entire
family. He rose to take the girls to practice from five until
eight in the morning, at which time he would take them
to school and he would go to work. "I told them, I don't
mind doing it, but you have to make a commitment. In
five years you can become a senior skater. We always had
that as the goal," Danny said.

In order to meet that goal, every six months Michelle
and Karen were taking the tests that would allow them to
move from one level to the next. The tests consisted of a
series of increasingly difficult moves that had to be successfully executed on the ice. For the most part, the sisters
were fairly equal in their abilities, although one would
occasionally move ahead a level before the other caught
up. But increased abilities meant more time was needed
to train for both girls. They were already skating five days
a week, and the rink at Torrance was not available on
weekends. Michelle and Karen would have to look else-
where to train.

Learning to Jump and Spin

In the 1980s figure skating was undergoing a change that shaped it into the sport we know today. The name *figure skating* was originally derived from the patterns skaters had to trace on the ice. Variations of figure eights, also known as *compulsory school figures,* required skaters to be diligent and patient as they carved out these shapes. Skaters' scores in competitions counted for a sizable share of the skater's final total. A skater, for example, could perform very well in the long program but still finish in second or third place (or lower) if she did not excel at the figures.

When Michelle first began skating, compulsory school figures were still a part of skating, although by the mid-1980s they were on their way out. By 1991 they had been eliminated from the sport altogether, as skating started to look toward athletes who were able to jump as well as display a great deal of artistry. For this reason, skaters such as Michelle and Karen were coming along at a perfect time in which to quickly advance through skating's ranks. A few years earlier and they would have been required to learn the figures, by many accounts a tedious routine that often slowed down the progress of future stars.

Instead, as a young skater Michelle was able to concentrate on moves such as the Axel, an easily recognizable jump that takes off from a forward position and is so named for its creator, Axel Paulsen, and the Lutz, a toe-pick-assisted jump named for Alois Lutz that launches from the back outside edge, as well as numerous other spins and spirals. As Michelle and Karen mastered these and other moves, the question became where they would go to continue their training.

To Lake Arrowhead and Frank Carroll

In 1991, the Kwans discovered Ice Castle Training Center, a famous training facility located in the San Bernardino Mountains about 100 miles from Los Angeles in a town called Lake Arrowhead. At the center were two training spaces: a public facility that offered open skating every day of the week and a private rink at which many top-tiered skaters had trained. At first, Danny and Estella started bringing the girls to Ice Castle on week-ends so that they could train while the Torrance rink was occupied.

Michelle and Karen continued to compete and advance in the ranks, and by 1992 both were skating at the junior level—just one step away from the senior ranking. That year proved to be a milestone for Michelle. After winning a gold medal in a regional juniors competition, she continued to a sectionals event in which she captured the bronze. That win made Michelle eligible for her first national competition: the Junior Nationals.

Michelle was happy with the way that she had been skating, but the Kwans had not been able to afford a coach for more than nine months. The family had been receiving some money from friends and supporters of the young skaters, but it was not enough to cover the cost of a coach. So, as Michelle began to prepare for her first national competition, it seemed as if she might have to go it alone—until a miraculous intervention occurred.

Virginia Fratianne, the mother of 1980s Olympic skater Linda Fratianne, introduced the Kwans to Frank Carroll, a respected coach who had instructed her daughter, among other young champions. Carroll, a former competitive skater himself, worked at Ice Castle, and Virginia arranged for both girls to have a lesson with him so that he could see whether or not he wanted to work with them. With the Junior Nationals only three weeks away, Michelle was incredibly nervous as she approached her "audition" with Carroll. "I wasn't sure if I belonged with the top skaters Frank coached, but something inside me told me that I might," she said.

After witnessing her lesson, Carroll agreed. In fact, he took on both Michelle and Karen as his students. He later told Michelle that the first time he watched her skate he knew she could be a world champion. But there would be many bumps on the road to the top.

Michelle trains with coach Frank Carroll. Carroll said that the first time he saw Michelle perform, he knew she could be a world champion. (Corbis)

The National Level

With Carroll as the Kwans' coach, everything started happening at a much faster pace. Michelle still had just a few weeks until the Junior Nationals, but the girls were about to undergo an immediate overhaul of the way they had been living. Through the assistance of Carroll and Virginia

Fratianne, Michelle and Karen were granted scholarships that would enable them to study at Ice Castle's private rink. They would eat and sleep at the facility and go to school in nearby Lake Arrowhead. They would be living the skating life every day.

But something happened as Michelle began preparing for Junior Nationals with Carroll. Once at Ice Castle, surrounded by many other talented and dedicated skaters, she realized that she had many bad habits that would have to be corrected. For example, Carroll quickly taught her the importance of picking herself up and continuing with her program after a fall. In a competition that is what she would have to do, and her new coach emphasized the importance of doing the same thing in practice. She also started to concentrate on her consistency. If she was not able to successfully complete a jump four out of five times in practice, Carroll would remove it from her program until she could get it right. Michelle would later say that she thought she was disciplined when she got to Ice Castle, but the fact was she had a lot to learn.

Still, Michelle was eager to participate in her first national competition. She had performed so well in the regional and sectional events that she assumed she would be able to continue winning right on into the nationals. Nonetheless, Michelle continued to practice hard. She was pushing herself so much that one night, as the big event approached, Danny Kwan overheard his young daughter talking in her sleep. "It's nothing, it's nothing" she repeated, while trying to calm herself as she dreamed about skating. Danny, who often drove the two hours from the family's home to spend the night with his daughters, was overcome with guilt. Later he would ask himself, "What am I doing to her?"

On the day of the contest, which was held in Florida, Michelle realized for the first time the level of competition she would be facing. For one thing, the skating levels were tied to ability, not age; there was no maximum or minimum age at which an athlete could enter a level. So skaters could be much older and still compete in the junior level. But at 11 years old, Michelle was one of the youngest juniors on the ice.

And then it was Michelle's turn to skate. She would later describe both her long and short programs as "disasters." "It was nothing like at the sectionals, where everything had gone so smoothly. Here, everything went wrong. It was a shock to me," she wrote. Michelle finished in ninth place. "Afterward I cried like a baby," she says.

Michelle would come to realize that she had been feeling too confident about her abilities. She knew it, and she suspected her coach knew it as well. She thought Frank Carroll had given her an opportunity to see just how difficult national competition is by letting her get a little bit overconfident. But the growing pains between student and teacher were not over. Even though she had fared poorly at the Junior Nationals, Michelle knew she could skate so much better. She had been working hard for nearly five years. Now she just needed another chance to prove herself.

On to the Next Level

Nearly four years had passed since Michelle saw Brian Boitano win his medal at the 1988 Olympics. After the 1992 Games in Barcelona, Spain, it was decided that the summer and winter Olympic Games would alternate every two years. Until then, both games had been held at the same time every four years. But the only skaters chosen for the Olympic team were senior-level skaters. So now, with the 1994 Winter Games rapidly approaching, Michelle knew that if she hoped to compete she would have to take the test to advance to the senior level. Plus, nearly five years had passed—the amount of time in which she had promised her father she would advance to the seniors.

There was one small problem: Frank Carroll was absolutely opposed to the idea. According to Carroll, if Michelle stayed at the junior level for another year, she would stand a better chance of advancing quickly as she made herself more known to the judges. Judges, Carroll

At the age of 12, the fiercely competitive Michelle had already attained the title of senior skater. (Corbis)

told her, like to see skaters who have paid their dues instead of those who have risen through the ranks too fast. Plus, Karen was not quite ready to move up to the next level, either. But Michelle convinced herself that she was ready to become a senior.

Since she knew Frank was against the idea, she waited until he was out of town at a coaches' conference. Then she told her dad—who wasn't aware that Frank did not want her to advance—that she was ready to take the test. They went to Los Angeles, where Michelle passed her program in front of a panel of judges. With that, Michelle Kwan had reached the title of senior skater. And she was not yet 12 years old.

3

A TASTE OF SUCCESS

Despite passing her senior test with ease, Michelle's move to skating's big leagues did not get off to an easy start. For one thing, she had to tell Frank Carroll that she had ignored his advice and taken the test against his wishes. He did not take the news well.

"He flipped his lid," Michelle wrote in her 1997 autobiography. "He was furious. For a few days he wouldn't talk to me." It was, Michelle later admitted, one of the few times that she had disregarded the wisdom of someone older and wiser than herself. Danny Kwan called it "an honest mistake. . . . We'd only known Frank four months, and I thought Michelle had told him about [the test]. The only thing she wanted was to be a senior and compete against the big guys," Kwan told one journalist.

Frank's concern was not that Michelle could not technically compete at the senior level. He was concerned that Michelle did not understand what was required of a skater artistically. The pressure, he assured his student, would be tremendous, and every aspect of her skating—from her appearance to her footwork—would need work. At first her parents were a little worried about what lay ahead for Michelle. But when they saw how badly she wanted to succeed, they were there beside her as they always had been. And now, there was no turning back.

Rising to the Challenge

True, Michelle had plenty to learn. But in her first year as a senior skater, she proved that she was up to the task. Michelle won first place in the Southwest Pacific Regional and in the Pacific Coast Sectional. Now she had qualified for her first national competition as a senior skater. In early 1993, she headed to Phoenix, that year's site of the event, to skate with her idols.

There, Michelle was skating alongside athletes such as Nancy Kerrigan and reigning U.S. champion Tonya Harding, both of whom would play a major role in Michelle's rise to the top in the following years. In Phoenix, Michelle warmed up next to Harding and was a little bit awed by the champ's triple Axels. In the competition, Michelle followed Harding on the ice. Although she missed a couple of jumps, Michelle's performance was not a total disaster. She finished in sixth place—a respectable showing for the 12-year-old girl. "I felt sure that if I kept working, I could do a lot better next year," she said.

The rest of the 1992–93 season provided valuable—and fun—experiences for Michelle. She made her first trip overseas, skating in an event called the Gardena Spring Trophy in Italy, and later she appeared at the Olympic Festival event in San Antonio, Texas, where she performed in front of 25,000 roaring fans—and was the youngest skater to ever win the event. Michelle was on her way to becoming one of "the big guys."

A Skating Season

Unlike other sports, figure skating's "season" is not clearly defined. It is not like baseball, where teams play every few days, or even tennis, where there are many tournaments throughout the season. But skating does have some key events. For American skaters there is the National Championships, which take place in January or February. This is the beginning of the season's end for most skaters. The World Championships follow Nationals in March, except during Winter Olympics years (2004, 2008, 2012, and so on). During Olympics years, the Games are sandwiched between the National and World Championships.

There are some competitions in the fall, and often-times skaters will perform with traveling ice shows after the Worlds event. But for the most part, skating is a lot of practice—alone on cold, often deserted rinks—broken up

Michelle competed with some of the biggest names in skating at the U.S. National competition in 1993. (WireImage)

by a few competitions. In order to succeed, figure skaters have to want something more than just performing in front of enthusiastic audiences.

This fact has not been lost on Michelle. From the earliest point in her career, she was seeking much more than a cheering crowd. Being a successful skater, she said, began as a dream. Michelle described her early fascination with the sport, and her dream, in her 1999 motivational book, *The Winning Attitude*: "Once you've seen your dream, it will begin to take on a life of its own. With luck, it will grow stronger and stronger," she wrote. "Some days it will be stronger than you. You'll need it, believe me. When you're feeling lazy or blue or things aren't going so great, it'll get you out of bed and out the door. It will *motivate* you to keep going."

As Michelle's competitions became more serious and were held at distances that were farther away from Lake Arrowhead, she had to devote an increasing amount of time to her practices. Senior skaters usually have three 45-minute practices on the ice per day, along with some additional weight training or other exercise, and hours spent planning new routines. Michelle was no exception, and the days were long and demanding. Plus, she still had to keep up with her schoolwork. She had always been an A student, and until the eighth grade she had attended classes with the other kids. But now she started to work with a tutor because it became apparent that she would not be able to skate at this level and go to school during the usual hours. "I like my schedule to be jam-packed," she told a reporter. "I didn't want to finish my homework and watch four hours of TV. I wanted to get to the 1994 Olympics."

The Beginning of an Olympic Dream

Frank Carroll may not have been as focused on getting Michelle in the 1994 Winter Games as she was with going, but he was intent on turning his pupil into the best skater she could be. Carroll's training program was a rigid one, and Michelle learned a number of things right from the start. For one thing, her coach insisted that during practice she continue through a program no matter what the circumstances, even if she fell down in the middle of it.

Carroll's philosophy was that if Michelle made a mistake and tripped or fell during a practice program, then that was a perfect opportunity for her to test how she would recover from that accident. "If you let that opportunity go by," Carroll said, "then you have not practiced that possibility of something happening." He expected Michelle to be able to hit a jump at least 80 percent of the time in practice or it would not go into her performance routine. He was pushing Michelle and she was living up to his expectations. Then, something happened that not only rocked the figure skating world, but also changed Michelle's career for good.

In 1994, the National Championships were held in Detroit. Michelle, now 13 years old, was once again competing with skaters whose styles had influenced her as she was coming up in the ranks. Nancy Kerrigan, the defending U.S. champion, was 24 years old, and Tonya Harding, a powerful skater and longtime idol of Michelle's, was 23. Late in 1993, Michelle had competed in the World Junior Championships—her last chance to do so—where she finished in first place. But with the National Championships, as well as future World Championships, she would be competing at a much higher level. Michelle knew that she had her work cut out for her. Karen Kwan had since advanced to the senior level as well, but she had failed to qualify for Nationals. However, as Michelle was preparing for the contest, Karen recounted a vivid dream she had in which Nancy Kerrigan bowed out of the competition and Michelle finished in second place.

Days later the dream turned out to be eerily prophetic when, following a practice session in Detroit, Kerrigan was struck on the leg by an unknown assailant. Michelle had been practicing on the same ice as Nancy when Kerrigan stepped off the rink. Someone called to the champion skater, who then disappeared behind a curtain that cordoned off the backstage area. Kerrigan then screamed, and people rushed to her aid. It was later discovered that Kerrigan was hit by a friend of Tonya Harding's husband in an effort to stop Kerrigan from competing in the 1994 Winter Olympics, which were only days away.

No one knew of the plot at the time, and Kerrigan was forced to withdraw from the National Championships. As unfortunate as her absence was, it turned out to help Michelle, who finished second in the Nationals, right behind Harding. In addition, Nationals served as the trial run for the Olympics. If Nancy was not able to compete, it was likely that 13-year-old Michelle Kwan, now the second-ranked skater in the United States, would be taking her place.

The sad truth about Kerrigan's attack unfolded rather quickly. It soon became clear that Tonya Harding had played some role in this reprehensible act, but what she knew was not immediately apparent. Thankfully, Kerrigan's injuries were not nearly as severe as they could have been. But the Olympics were about to begin in Lillehammer, Norway, and the Olympic committee had to decide which skaters to send to the Games. Under normal circumstances, the first- and second-place finishers in Nationals would advance to the Olympics. But the committee was reluctant to deny Kerrigan a spot even though she was unable to skate at Nationals. And Harding—

although her career would soon be over—had not yet been found guilty of any wrongdoing. It was decided that Kerrigan and Harding would skate in the Olympics, but Michelle was going along as an alternate.

Ultimately Michelle's role in Lillehammer would be small, as she lived and practiced apart from the other skaters. But the experience turned out to be educational nonetheless. For starters, it was Michelle's first real exposure to the media, who covered the Kerrigan-Harding drama from top to bottom—and that included getting to know Michelle Kwan. The pressure was so intense that her parents ended up hiring a sports agent to manage her. And, with her typically rosy outlook, Michelle did note that she had achieved her earlier goal of making it to these Games. "I was in the stands watching and not on the ice skating rink, but technically speaking, my dream did come true," she later wrote.

Front and Center on the World Stage

That attention prior to the '94 Olympics was not the reason for which Michelle had wanted to be noticed. But that was about to change. After Kerrigan's disappointing finish at the Games (she took the silver medal to Ukrainian skater Oksana Baiul's gold) and Harding's total washout (she left amateur skating soon after), both of America's top skaters decided against competing in the World Championships, just weeks away in Chiba, Japan.

At 13, Michelle would be the youngest skater to ever compete for the U.S. team. As if that pressure was not enough, in order to guarantee two spots for the following year's American team, Michelle would have to finish at least in the top 10. Barely a teenager, Michelle Kwan would have to demonstrate that she belonged among the world's figure-skating elite.

When Frank Carroll had protested Michelle's advancement to the senior level, it was not only because he wanted to see his student get more experience. Carroll was also aware that judges had a certain way of looking at skaters, regardless of that skater's ability. Judges traditionally liked a certain sense of maturity in winning skaters. Michelle was a promising skater but still a young girl, and one word would be used to describe her again and again: cute. Judges were looking for a "lady" senior skater, someone who projected the aura of a mature, seasoned athlete—not a cute, young girl.

But part of the problem was that Michelle was exactly that: a cute, young skater. She was four-foot-nine inches tall and weighed less than 100 pounds. At that age she took to the ice in pretty but girlish costumes and without makeup, which was in keeping with her parents' traditional Chinese customs. With her hair in a ponytail and wearing a necklace from her grandmother intended to bring good luck (which she never removes), Michelle was in all respects a young girl, even if she was competing with the top skaters in the world.

As Carroll prepared Michelle for the competition in Japan, the pair had their work cut out for them. Carroll enlisted the help of skating legend Irina Rodnina, an Olympic and World pairs skater, to help train Michelle. "We desperately need to pump me up—to make the judges believe that I was more than *cute*, that I was mature and good enough to rank in the top 10 in the world," Michelle later wrote.

Kerrigan and Harding may have been absent from the event, but the lineup of skaters she would be competing against was, to Michelle, a who's who of the best figure skaters. When she entered the arena in Japan, Michelle saw skaters such as Lu Chen, the Chinese skater who had captured the bronze medal in Lillehammer, and Surya Bonaly, the European champion from France. It was then that the magnitude of the event hit her. She thought, "I'm competing against *them*?"

Michelle's short program was not particularly memorable. She had some trouble with her triple Lutz, but considering the fact that none of the judges had ever seen her skate before—there were no American judges on the panel—she was in 11th place after the first event. The long program, which counted for two-thirds the total score, was a couple days away. Michelle would have to improve on her showing in order to finish in the top 10, and she would need to complete two planned triple Lutzes in her long program in order to do so.

Rating the Jumps

The triple Lutz is considered one of the most difficult jumps, second only to the triple Axel. The other jumps, which require the skater to take off from her toe, follow in decreasing difficulty, including the triple flip and the triple toe loop. Jumps that originate from the back edge such as the loop and the Salchow, named for Swedish skater Ulrich Salchow, are generally considered easier. Jumps can be done singly, or as a double or triple, with the triple move being the most difficult.

For a short program, a skater is required to perform a set number of moves, including one jump combination; several spins, which require the skater to twirl on the ice; a spiral sequence, which demonstrates the skater's flexibility and fluidity; and a series of footwork steps that illustrate her precision and dexterity. Extra jumps are worth additional points, but the program is only two minutes long. The rest of the elements must be included or points will be deducted from the skater's total. In addition, if the skater makes a mistake while attempting one of these maneuvers during the program, she cannot attempt it again. The short program's emphasis on ability is why it is known as the technical program.

The long program allows the skater much more leeway in what she presents. Skaters can make substitutions to their routines without it counting against their point total, and jumps or spins that do not go as planned can be retried. The emphasis in the artistic program is on the skater as a whole: not only how she completes her moves, but also how she looks doing so, how she combines her routine with her music, the judges' overall impression of her, and many other factors.

So when Michelle took to the ice for the long program at her first World Championship, she knew what she had to do. First, she had to stay calm and focus on her skating. Carroll gave her a pep talk as she was preparing to go out onto the ice, and once in the center of the rink in her starting pose, she "felt like the world was on [her] side." Michelle was trying to project herself as a mature, serious skater, and the crowd around her was cheering her on. Then, something that rarely happened occurred—Michelle broke into a smile. "The pressure was on, and I liked it," she later wrote. "This was the kind of attention and challenge I wanted."

And Michelle lived up to her own expectations. She completed both triple Lutzes and a perfect double Axel.

There were a few small errors, including a step between a jump combination in which one of her feet touched down, and a moment where her hand grazed the ice as she attempted to keep herself from falling. But overall the routine from the Worlds newcomer was an impressive feat. The crowd started clapping wildly, and one fan threw a cowboy hat onto the ice, which Michelle put on her head as she skated to the "Kiss and Cry," the area where coaches and their skaters gather after a performance to await their score. It was so named because skaters first kissed their coaches upon completing a routine, and then they cried—either tears of joy or tears of sorrow.

Michelle had done it; she had delivered a stunning long program for a first-time Worlds entrant. In the stands, her parents cheered as other audience members echoed their applause. However, when the scores were revealed, Michelle's marks were lower than might have been expected. While she did all right on the technical aspect of the program, her artistic scores were so-so. But this is the nature of world-class figure skating. For Michelle, a new face for all these judges, had nothing with which to compare herself against. Still, her performance and scores were good enough to elevate her into the top 10 and guarantee that two U.S. skaters would attend next year's World Championships. Michelle Kwan was now ranked eighth in the world.

The rest of 1994 suddenly became very busy for Michelle. With her eighth-place showing at Worlds, she was asked to skate in pro-am competitions, in which professional skaters compete against amateurs. She was also invited to join the Campbell's Soups Tour of World Figure Skating Champions, one of the professional ice shows that travel from city to city. With the tour, Michelle performed 76 shows that summer, alongside skaters such as Nancy Kerrigan, Oksana Baiul, and her inspiration, Brian Boitano, with whom she spent much of her off time working on moves like her triple Axel. That year she also competed in the Goodwill Games, Skate America, and the Hershey's Kisses U.S. Pro-Am Championships, at which Michelle won the silver medal and took home a $30,000 prize.

But more than anything she was looking ahead to the next National and World Championships. Michelle had scored two spots for the U.S. team at the World Championships, but in order to be one of the skaters to attend, she had to win at the Nationals.

Gaining Her Footing

The 1995 Nationals would be held in Providence, Rhode Island. Based on Michelle's performances throughout the year, many skating fans thought she stood a good chance to win. More people than ever were tuning into the sport that year, following the Nancy Kerrigan–Tonya Harding story. But these Nationals, which marked the end of the 1994–95 season, would have significance for Michelle in more ways than one. To begin with, Karen Kwan had also qualified for the competition, which meant that the Kwan sisters would be competing in the senior Nationals for the first time. It was also the first time two sisters had gone head-to-head at Nationals since 1959.

For Michelle, the fact that she was competing against her sister just meant that she was happy her sister would be by her side. The media tried to play up the idea of sibling rivalry between Michelle and Karen, but from the sisters' viewpoint there was no rivalry. "Being together at Nationals just made it all so much more fun," Michelle said.

Besides, Michelle had other things to focus on. That everyone was labeling her the "favorite" began to put an undue amount of pressure on the young skater. Now 14, Michelle was suddenly becoming aware that many skating observers expected even more from her than she expected from herself. People were already anointing her the 1998 Olympic hopeful, even though she had yet to win a national event.

Michelle was facing some stiff competition, too: Tonia Kwiatkowski, a steady but unremarkable skater who was about to turn 24, and Nicole Bobek, a young, extremely talented athlete who had toured on the ice show with Michelle that summer. Despite Bobek's formidable talents on the ice, she was considered difficult to work with and a bit of a wild card.

The short program proved to be a tight one between the top three competitors, but a misstep on her triple-Lutz/double-toe combination left Michelle in third place at its completion. For the long program, Kwan was the last performer in the last group of performers, meaning that she had to wait some 45 minutes from the start of the pro-gram—and her warm-up—until it was her turn to take the ice. For a skater, there is little to do while the others per-form. Scores are usually broadcast over the loudspeakers, and those who skate toward the end usually must sit and endure until their time. Some listen to music, but Michelle tries to imagine herself performing a flawless program. Bobek had skated immediately before Michelle, and although Nicole had had a good routine, she had made a few mistakes that might have allowed Michelle to score higher.

At first everything went according to plan for Kwan. She landed the triple Lutz (her first of two) that had thwarted her in the short program. A triple flip jump fol-lowed, and she made a beautiful recovery on a triple toe loop. But going into her final triple Lutz she sensed some-thing was wrong. "Before I even took off into the air I knew I would fall," she later wrote. And she did, crashing onto the ice on her hip. She quickly got up and completed her program, faring nearly as well as Bobek, but not quite. For the second time, Michelle was the Nationals' silver-medal winner. Karen finished in seventh place. But Michelle's second-place finish still meant she, along with Nicole Bobek, was headed to the World Championships.

"I'd never skated better."

The international competition in 1995 was to be held in Birmingham, England. After Michelle's showing at Nationals, it became clear to Frank Carroll that there would have to be some changes to his student's routine. Carroll started by replacing some of Michelle's easier jumps with moves that were more difficult for the young skater. The idea was that if Michelle could complete the more difficult jumps, she would earn more points on the technical aspect of her routines. "I wanted to go for doing the most difficult short program we could to try to get the highest first marks we could at Worlds," Carroll said.

Michelle's life was already difficult. She spent nearly three hours a day, every day, practicing on the ice. In addition, she trained with weights, took dance lessons, monitored her diet, and spent several hours each day with a tutor in order to keep up with her studies. But she proved herself up to the challenge.

When she took the ice for the short program in Birmingham, Michelle skated perfectly. She was the eighth skater out of 31, and she immediately followed the French champion Surya Bonaly. The contrast between Bonaly and Kwan was remarkable, notes author Christine Brennan in *Inside Edge*, her history of the 1994–95 season. Bonaly, a five-time European champion, faltered on four of the eight elements in her program. By comparison, Michelle did not make a single mistake. Yet Bonaly's scores were higher than Michelle's. "The judges obviously were looking at that résumé: World silver medalist and two-time Olympic hopeful," Brennan wrote. "Had a newcomer skated so poorly, she would have been near the bottom."

When Michelle saw her low scores, she asked Carroll if they were correct. "I was seriously confused," she wrote in her autobiography. "I'd never skated better." The crowd agreed, booing the judges' decisions. But Carroll understood what Michelle did not yet grasp: in the eyes of the judges, she was still just a cute, young girl. At the end of the short program, Michelle was in fifth place.

Once again Michelle was skating last in the long program. As Michelle was about to take the ice wearing a cute red-and-pink dress with her hair in a ponytail and no discernible makeup, Carroll whispered some words of encouragement to his 14-year-old student; he told her to

Michelle's fourth-place performance at the 1995 World Championships motivated her to work for the professional recognition she deserved. (Getty Images)

"sparkle." And that's what Michelle Kwan did. She hit one triple jump after another, aced both her triple Lutzes, and then added a double toe loop to her second Lutz. Smiling more than she ever had on the ice, as she neared the end of her program the tears began pouring down her face. The crowd went wild, awarding her the only standing ovation that night. But to the judges, she did not merit a medal. They gave her fourth place.

Growing Up Gracefully

Michelle's finish at the 1995 World Championships proved to be a turning point for the young skater. Kwan now understood that she had skated the best she possibly could, and still she did not get the recognition she deserved. It was not her fault, she knew, nor was it specifically the fault of the judges. Michelle was a great jumper and an amazingly athletic skater. But if she wanted to advance to the ranks of the world champions, she would have to do and be more than just a great athlete. She would have to take her skating to an entirely different level. "As a kid skater, I'd gone as far as I could. Now I needed to find Michelle, the Lady skater—the artist. For once, I didn't need Frank to tell me what to do next," she wrote.

Kwan would soon be 15 years old, and if she wanted to compete at the same level as other women skaters, she would have to be taken seriously as a woman. "They want a ladies' world champion, not a girls' world champion," Carroll said. Until now, Michelle had taken the ice and presented a pretty straightforward program that focused on her skating ability. Michelle had offered little in the way of musical or artistic interpretation.

But she knew that people—fans and judges—were thinking of her as a young skater. With that in mind, she approached Carroll and choreographer Lori Nichol and told them she wanted to work on her "artistic" side.

Michelle had been undergoing other changes as well. As she got older, she continued to grow and her body changed in many ways. She grew from four-foot-nine to four-eleven, to finally five-foot-two inches. And she added weight to her hips and her chest, pushing her from 88 pounds in 1994 to 105 pounds a few years later. But it was not just her body that was changing. As Michelle grew older, she was experiencing emotional changes as well. The thoughts and ideas and emotions that had shaped her as a girl were giving way to more mature thoughts and emotions. Her feelings, she said, were getting increasingly complicated. And she wanted her skating to reflect that. The challenge now was to find a way to combine her innate athleticism with an artistic program that would show the world a grown-up skater.

The Look of a Mature Skater

It was Lori Nichol's job to help select the music that Michelle skated to, and it was she and Frank Carroll who picked a piece from *Salome*, a one-act opera by the German composer Richard Strauss. The story, originally taken from the New Testament in the Bible, was rewritten by playwright Oscar Wilde, for whom Strauss composed the music. The biblical story tells the tale of a young dancer who performs the dance of the seven veils for Herod Antipas. In exchange for her performance, Herod presents the dancer with the head of John the Baptist. Michelle, in the role of Salome, would have to undergo a tremendous transformation from the "cute, young girl" whose perfect routines had failed to win over the judges at the 1995 World Championships.

If playing Salome required a more mature person, then stepping into those shoes was a challenge that Michelle met head-on. And the role had a liberating effect on her as well. As she started to become the character, a change crept over Michelle. "I was still 15 and just a kid, but Salome started to bring out another more mature person," she wrote in *Heart of a Champion*. "Off the ice I wasn't really so different, just a little taller and a little rounder here and there. But on the ice, I had grown up."

But it was not just a new role that Michelle was assuming. She would have to have a new look as well—an older, more mature look. That meant she would have to lose the ponytail and the girlish costumes, and she would also have to start wearing some makeup. All the changes, especially the makeup, required some convincing of Michelle's parents. No mother or father likes to see her or his little girl grow up too fast, but the Kwans understood that skating was the road that Michelle had taken. And Danny and Estella Kwan knew that if Michelle wanted to win in what was a mature division, she would have to be viewed as a mature skater.

Michelle debuted her new role in October 1995 at Skate America, the first of several Olympic-style competitions in the 1995–96 season that were called the Champion Series. These events allowed skaters to earn prize money without forfeiting their Olympic eligibility. When Michelle took to the ice, it was the first time she had skated in front of a crowd in several months. Her hair was piled in a bun that had been braided and was held in place atop her head. She wore a deep, brilliant shade of red lipstick, makeup, and an elegant dress. Indeed, she had an entirely new persona.

With a new short program, "Spanish Medley," Michelle demonstrated that she was no longer the little girl fans had watched the past couple years. But it was not until she unveiled "Salome" for her long program that the audience truly grasped just how much she had changed. Gone was the perky, flawless jumper who had amazed audiences with her athletic ability. In her place was a graceful, sophisticated skater, who combined her perfect execution with a creative and mesmerizing artistic interpretation. Michelle beat China's Lu Chen to capture first place in Skate America, but it was only the beginning.

A Champion at Last

That season, 15-year-old Michelle entered more competitions than she ever had before. With each performance, she became just a bit more comfortable as Salome. She took first place at several of those contests including Skate Canada and the Nations Cup, but for Michelle these were just preludes to the big year-end competitions. This would be the young skater's fourth trip to Nationals and this time, she thought, it was going to be different. Yes, she had been ready during her previous trips, but at each event she had been in awe of the other skaters. She had felt, she later wrote, that she didn't belong with "the older, more experienced women skaters." But now she was one of those skaters, and she had no doubts about her ability to win the gold.

The 1996 National Championships were held in San Jose, California, and Michelle and her sister, Karen, would once again be competing together in the national event. Michelle's main competition was expected to come from

Nicole Bobek, but after a beautiful short program, Michelle led the pack and Nicole was in third. Finally, for the long program, Michelle performed an error-free "Salome" that wowed the audience. After two consecutive silver-medal finishes, Michelle Kwan won the National Championships, becoming the youngest skater to do so since Peggy Fleming in 1964. Karen finished in fifth place. Bobek had withdrawn from the long program because of a sore ankle, but there was a new skater who had made an impressive third-place finish that year: 13-year-old Tara Lipinski.

The results of Nationals meant that Michelle, second-place finisher Tonia Kwiatkowski, and Lipinski would be headed to Edmonton in Alberta, Canada, to compete in the World Championships. Michelle was about to find out if she could overcome the previous year's disappointing finish in England.

Suffering from a bad cold and some difficult practice sessions, Michelle still managed a somewhat surprising victory at the Champions Series Final in Paris before heading to Edmonton. Once in Canada, any difficulty she'd had in Paris simply evaporated. Many spectators were predicting stiff competition from Lu Chen, the reigning world champion, and Japan's 1992 Olympic silver-medal winner Midori Ito, who had returned to the amateur-skating world, but even before Michelle performed, something felt right about her being in Canada. "What I felt at Nationals, I felt even more strongly at Edmonton—that *my* best could be *the* best," she said.

Michelle was ahead after the short program, but the true test was about to begin. In order to focus on her upcoming performance, Michelle and Frank Carroll hid out backstage. Lu Chen skated before Michelle, and even though she and Carroll weren't watching, they heard the judges' scores over the public address system: They included two perfect 6.0s. It was the first time Michelle could recall any skater getting a perfect score at Worlds, and she began to get worried. But in addition to Lu Chen's sixes, a couple of judges had given her 5.8s. Carroll tried to get his skater ready for her long program. "I had about two seconds to say something intelligent and meaningful before she had to go out and skate," Carroll later told a reporter. "So I told her those were fabulous marks, but the judges had left room for her to win."

Michelle knew that was the truth. She skated to the center of the ice in her Salome costume, and as the music started, Michelle felt it wash over her. This role, this new performance, was everything she had thought it could be. Her long program was going perfectly, but as she neared the end of it she remembered that Lu Chen had received two perfect scores. Even though Michelle had not made any mistakes, she knew that if she wanted to win she was

Michelle proudly displays her gold medal at the 1996 World Figure Skating Championships. (Associated Press)

going to have to do something that would set her apart from Chen. A last-minute adjustment turned her final double Axel into a triple toe loop, giving her one more triple jump than Lu Chen, and she had not made any mistakes. When the scores were read, she had seven 5.9s for presentation and two 6.0s of her own.

Michelle was the new world champion.

4

THE TOP— AND THE BOTTOM

Michelle's victory at the '96 World Championships kicked her career into high gear. There were interviews and television appearances and fan letters—and more events. She took it all in stride; in fact, some people thought she handled it a little too easily. When asked if she was surprised that she had won the world championship at such a young age (only Sonja Henie, a skater from the 1920s, and Oksana Baiul were younger than Kwan when they won), Michelle said no. That answer, she wrote in her autobiography, may have sounded a little arrogant. "But the fact was that I wasn't surprised. That's not the word for it. Excited, overwhelmed, happy: yes. But ever since I was seven, I had imagined myself as a championship skater."

There was, however, a downside to being on top. Once you are there, there is no place to go but down. You can either hold on to what you have, or someone else will take it from you. But you cannot go any higher. Danny Kwan had repeated this lesson to his daughter many times.

Following Worlds, the year 1996 was off to a good enough start. Once again Michelle joined the Campbell's Soups Tour, and she was out on the road most of the summer. The tour traveled from city to city by bus, and Estella Kwan rode with her daughter along the way. Michelle also had struck a fast friendship with Harris Collins, the stage manager of the tour. Despite being more than 30 years older than Michelle, she and Harris clowned around like high school friends.

For Michelle, the tour was a good way to unwind after the intensity of the National and World Championships. Not only was it a chance for her to spend time with her mom, but she was able to be with many skaters whom she admired. Despite winning the Worlds—which many of the skaters on the tour had previously done themselves—Michelle did not receive any special treatment from them. To this group, she was just "Shelley." But the 1996 tour took a tragic turn one evening when, prior to the start of a show, Collins collapsed backstage. Michelle did not find out until later that the 49-year-old stage manager had died of a heart attack.

Collins's death was a sad blow to the tour and its skaters, but it also marked a difficult turning point in Michelle's career. She and Harris had been good friends, and his passing was a particularly difficult occurrence for her. When she received the news, "I suddenly realized how *young* 49 years old was," she wrote in *Heart of a Champion*. It was one of a number of things that, through the year, began to erode the pedestal Michelle had fought her way to the top of.

The Difficult Road to the '97 Nationals

Through the rest of 1996, it did not seem to most of the world that Michelle would have any trouble defending her national or world title. She won several competitions, including the Trophée Lalique in Paris, during which she demonstrated new short and long programs. For both programs, Michelle adapted a couple of interesting characters whose stories were set to music: for the short program she played Desdemona, the wife of the title character in Shakespeare's *Othello*. The long was based on Mumtaz Mahal, the favorite wife of India's Shah Jahan, for whom the Taj Mahal temple was built in the 1600s. On the surface, both programs were as beautiful and as stunning as "Salome." But what was going on inside of Michelle was not as apparent.

In addition to suffering the loss of her friend, Michelle was fighting several other personal battles as well. Her sister and longtime training partner, Karen, had moved across the country to start school at Boston University. Her brother, Ron, had left home several years earlier for school, and now that the family could afford a new house, Michelle was coming home to an empty place. She started to have a lot of problems with her skates, which required numerous adjustments from her father, and the practices that Michelle once looked forward to suddenly became a chore. Her response? She started to work harder than ever.

As the 1997 Nationals edged closer, Michelle's tension grew. She had won six other events since her appearance at the 1996 competition, and she was a favorite to capture this one as well. However, she did not see it that way. As the date for the competition in Nashville drew near, Michelle got increasingly anxious. "Everybody says, 'You're on a roll,'" she said. "It doesn't feel like it." She tried to put those thoughts out of her head, and she smiled as she told reporters she was just going to go out and have fun.

A New Kid on the Block

Once again, both Michelle and Karen would be competing at Nationals. Karen had not focused on skating as much since enrolling at Boston University, but she had performed well enough to skate her way into the U.S.

Championships. It was a great help to be competing with her sister, but Michelle still had not been able to shake the bad feelings and poor practices she had been having. As the event got under way, Michelle was one of the first skaters to perform in the short program. She had become accustomed to performing later, after the competition had been on for a while. However, Michelle still delivered a great program. After everyone had skated she was in first place, followed by Tara Lipinski in second and Tonia Kwiatkowski in third.

On the ice for her long program, in front of thousands of fans and millions of TV viewers, Michelle looked positively radiant in her red-and-gold costume. Her performance was off to a perfect start with a flying camel spin, in which the skater's free leg is extended behind her at a 90-degree angle to the ice, followed by a triple-triple toe-loop combination. As she came down into the landing of the second jump, something happened. She had landed on the side of her blade and her leg went out from under her. The sure-footed Michelle Kwan went sprawling across the ice. She regained her footing, stumbled, and fell again. She would nearly fall again in what was her most disastrous long program ever. But then, in the midst of it, the crowd started clapping, giving Michelle the strength to make it through her four-minute performance.

Michelle stumbles during her routine at the 1997 U.S. Championships. (Getty Images)

In the end, her program had not been a total bust. Michelle's scores ranged from 5.3 to 5.7 for the technical performance and 5.6 to 5.9 for the artistic. Tara Lipinski, then 14 years old, followed Michelle with a flawless performance. Lipinski became the youngest skater ever to win the U.S. Nationals. Michelle took home the silver medal (and Karen Kwan finished in seventh place), but she had relinquished her title.

Later, Michelle would say that after first stumbling she panicked. But the fall did not come as a surprise to some of the people close to her—least of all to Michelle herself. For months she had kept having premonitions that she would fall. Try as she might, she could not rule out the "bad voices" that were telling her she was going to go down on the ice. Her friend and mentor Brian Boitano called a few days after the incident to ask how she was. Boitano said that he had seen the fear written on her face. He told her that she should not focus on what could go wrong during her program. Instead, she needed to imagine what would go right. Michelle knew that he was right. "That negative voice in my head had been blasting," she later wrote. "I had thought I could just ignore it, but somehow that had only made it louder."

Shortly after the program, Danny Kwan asked his daughter, "Well, Michelle, what did you learn from this?" That question had been a long time coming. Things had not been right for Michelle for much of the past year, but they were going to get worse before they got better.

Second Again . . . and Again

After Michelle's surprising falls at Nationals, people assumed she would return to form. Instead, just the opposite happened. At the Champions Series Final in Hamilton, Ontario, just a few weeks later, Michelle once again had trouble with her jumps and placed second to Lipinski. The skaters scarcely had any time to breathe before they were off to Lausanne, Switzerland, site of the 1997 World Championships.

Worlds had always been Michelle's favorite competition, but she might have had more than just a little apprehension coming into this year's event. With Lipinski having taken Kwan's national title and the Series Final away from her, the media was having a great time playing up the "rivalry" between the two skaters. At 16 years old, Michelle was the veteran. The question on everyone's mind was whether or not the young upstart Lipinski would be able to upset the experienced world champion Kwan.

As her short program began, Michelle thought that she had prepared herself as best she could. Despite her two recent losses to Lipinski, she believed that she was now in a positive place and would be able to defend her world title. Initially everything was going fine. But then, coming out of a jump, Michelle stumbled and put her other foot down, which resulted in a major point loss from the judges. By the time her two minutes were up, the thoughts of her earlier falls at Nationals had already swept through her head and she imagined herself going down again here. When the results of the short program were posted, Michelle was in fourth place.

Before Michelle could get too deep in self-pity, two things happened that brought her—and everyone in the skating world—back to earth. First, renowned skating coach Carlo Fassi, who had been working in Switzerland with Nicole Bobek, died suddenly of a heart attack in Lausanne. Bobek, who had been attempting to get her skating career back on track, had enlisted the legendary Fassi, the coach of Peggy Fleming, Dorothy Hamill, and many others. Fassi's death cast a pall over the competition, but remarkably his wife, Christa, stayed to coach Bobek through the long program.

The skaters had barely had time to process this news when another bombshell fell. Word spread that Olympic gold-medalist and four-time world champion Scott Hamilton was being treated for testicular cancer. Although the treatments for Hamilton's cancer were frequently successful and he was expected to recover fully, both tragedies shook Michelle to the core. Then, a strange thing happened. Michelle was putting on a pair of shoes and she was tying one of the laces. She had been thinking about Carlo and about Scott, and as she pulled back on one of her laces, it snapped and she hit herself in the face. "Suddenly I started laughing," she wrote in her autobiography. "I *needed* that whack in the head. What had I been thinking? Skating isn't a matter of life and death."

Michelle would later reflect on the period between her 1996 and 1997 World Championships as "the coma." But when she took the ice for the '97 Worlds long program, she was very much awake. As she flew over the ice, Michelle seemed to be experiencing all that had been absent from her performances that year. She was taking Brian Boitano's advice to heart and focusing not on what could go wrong, but what was going right. She seemed to love skating again, and for just a moment that was enough.

Michelle's long program at the 1997 World Championships was the best of the group. She knew it and the judges did too. But when it was tallied with her fourth-place showing in the short program, she came up second—Tara Lipinski was the new world champion. But to Michelle, that hardly mattered. She had a new perspective—one that would take her back to the top. "My wings were back," she wrote after her second-place finish. "Not a single tear fell. Some people said I was the happiest silver medalist they'd ever seen. I think they were right."

"It's good to have a rival."

At the end of the season Michelle returned home to Lake Arrowhead, determined to recapture the feelings that she had previously had about skating. Something had happened on her way to the top, and she needed to figure out what that was. After her devastating falls at Nationals, a confused Michelle had told her father, "Daddy, I have to learn to love the sport again." For his daughter, Danny Kwan said, skating had become all about winning or hanging on to what she had already won. She was worried that if she did not win, the fans would not like her. She was skating for all the wrong reasons.

At the onset of the 1996–97 season, Danny had listed for Michelle some aspects of her attitude and outlook that he thought she should work on. Among the areas he said she needed to work on: her perspective of the sport and her appreciation of the life she was leading. Danny continued to add to the list throughout the year, recalls Michelle, but instead of really working on these problems, she continued to push herself harder and harder on the rink, all the while fearful that she was going to fall or that something was going to go wrong. She called her buildup to Nationals a "dreadful time" and said, "[it] seemed like I had something to lose—more to lose than to gain." It took the loss of both her titles and the tragic circumstances of

Carlo Fassi and Scott Hamilton to help her regain what she had lost. "I learned a lot more when I was going downhill than when I was winning consecutive championships," she later admitted.

That summer, following the '97 Worlds, she once again joined Campbell's Soups Tour of World Figure Skating Champions. Michelle liked the ice tours for the ways in which they were different than skating in competitions. On tour, all eyes were on the skater, illuminated by a spotlight in the center of the rink in a darkened arena. During competitions, everything is lit up, and part of the skater's job is to look directly at the judges and make eye contact. But in the center of a show, the skater cannot see anyone or anything else. And, as in past years, the tour again allowed Michelle to spend time with old friends such as Brian Boitano. This year, however, there was another face on tour: Tara Lipinski.

It was the first chance the two rivals had to spend any time around one another outside of their competitions. While they did not become fast friends, they maintained a civil relationship, and Michelle later said that it was the pressure of Tara being right there that inspired her to work harder. "It's good to have a rival, to have someone pushing you, helping keep you in line," Michelle told one journalist. "Those days you skate badly or you're too tired and you just want to climb in bed. But you

Michelle's rival, Tara Lipinski. The competition between the two skaters only helped to improve their individual performances. (Associated Press)

think, 'I know she's out there working hard right now. I'd better get back to it.'"

Skating without Fear

Everything that Michelle had been through had changed her, but her trials were not over yet. In October Michelle, now 17, was given her first chance to compete since the World Championships in Switzerland. The event was Skate America in Detroit, and the tension was high as Michelle was once again scheduled to meet Tara on the ice. This time, however, Michelle said she was ready for it. She said she would skate forcefully and without fear—the emotion that had crippled her recent performances. And she did, easily beating Lipinski. But it was just a few weeks later at Skate Canada that she discovered the stress fracture in her left foot that would nearly sideline her from the 1998 National Championships in Philadelphia.

But Michelle bounced back from the injury and gave a historic performance in both the long and short programs at the 1998 Nationals. Michelle's coach liked to talk about her "core of metal." "Michelle is tough as nails," Frank Carroll said on more than one occasion. If ever there was a time to demonstrate that, proving her mettle at the '98 Nationals was that time, because the 1998 Winter Olympics were about to begin. That event would be

Michelle Kwan's chance to show the world that she had what it took to become an Olympian.

After her showing at Nationals in Philadelphia, Michelle was the overwhelming favorite to take the gold medal in Nagano, Japan. Thirty women skaters from 22 countries entered in the competition, but all eyes were on Michelle and Tara Lipinski. The two Americans were expected to capture the gold and silver medals, with Michelle taking the coveted top spot that she had dreamed of winning since she was seven years old.

Michelle later recalled when she first entered the Olympic arena in Japan: "I skated over the sign that said Nagano '98 Olympics. I had tears in my eyes just being at the Olympic building, being an Olympian." With the 15 scores of 6.0 she had amassed just weeks earlier at Nationals, many fans and commentators thought that all Michelle had to do in order to win the gold was success-fully complete both her programs without falling. Her only competition, they reasoned, would come from Lipinski. And the way that Michelle had been skating, it was believed that Tara's athletic but robotic style would be no match for Kwan's elegant performance.

But this competition, like Michelle's appearance the previous year at Worlds, would come with some bad news as well. While in Japan, she received word that her friend and Olympic skater Peggy Fleming had been diagnosed with breast cancer. Fleming, who had won the United States' only gold medal in the 1968 Olympics, spoke with Michelle by phone and urged the young skater to focus on the Games. "You have the Olympics to think about," Fleming, who has since recovered, told her. That is what Michelle tried to do.

An Olympic Letdown

Tara Lipinski took the ice first in the short program and skated very well. But Michelle's short program was even better, earning her scores of 5.9 from all nine judges for her artistic merit. At the end of the short program, Michelle was in the lead and Tara in second place. Later Michelle would say that during the warm-ups she was "a little overwhelmed," but the audience never would have known it.

Michelle was slotted to skate first in the long program. Once again she turned in a stunning performance. With the exception of a slight teeter in her step after landing a triple flip, Kwan's program was excellent and the judges awarded it as such with nine 5.9s for artistic merit. However, the wobbly landing left her with technical marks of 5.7s and 5.8s. Still, it should have been enough for Michelle to lock up the gold. In order for Lipinski to win, she would have to skate the program of a lifetime. And that is just what she did.

In contrast to the skilled but mechanical routines Tara Lipinski had come to be identified with, the 15-year-old skater delivered a fast-paced program that was both artistic and graceful. "I can't believe it! I was so good!" Tara said upon finishing her skate. The judges agreed. While she received a mix of 5.8s and 5.9s for her artistic presentation, her technical scores—six 5.9s and three 5.8s—put her ahead of Michelle overall. Tara Lipinski had won—by one-tenth of a point—and in doing so had become the youngest individual to win a Winter Olympics gold medal. It was also the United States' first gold-and-silver finish in women's figure skating since the 1956 Olympics.

Still, the loss was a devastating blow to Michelle, even though she did her best to keep it in perspective. "I came here to do a job. I worked very hard, I skated well," she told reporters afterward. "That's life. Working hard is no guarantee you're going to win the gold medal." Some critics speculated that Kwan might have been too reserved in her long program while Tara skated with abandon. Michelle agreed that she had been cautious because she did not want to make any mistakes. "This teaches me a lesson," she said. "I need to become free and enjoy the music and performance and let myself go."

5

BACK ON HER BLADES

The period immediately following the 1998 Olympics did not get much better for Michelle. After her win, Tara Lipinski decided to turn professional, thereby exempting her from the '98 World Championships that followed soon after in Minneapolis. The most pressing question for Michelle was whether or not she wanted to continue skating competitively. Ultimately, it was her coach Frank Carroll who urged her to continue. After Lipinski beat her at the Olympics, it was Carroll who was brutally honest with Michelle. While friends and family tried to blame the loss on poor judging, Carroll leveled with his student when he said, "You were wonderful, but it was not your greatest performance."

But at the 1998 World Championships in Minnesota, Michelle was left without any real competition after Tara's departure for the pro ranks. Regardless, it was not an easy win for Michelle. She was still suffering from the injury to her toe as well as throat and eye infections. Michelle managed to win but a couple mistakes, including a fall on a double Axel during her long program, hurt her score. She later admitted that during her performance she had to think very hard. "After I made two mistakes, I knew I had no more options but to do everything else," she said.

The Olympic Dream Lives On

After her victory at Worlds, Michelle announced that she would continue as an amateur until the 2002 Winter Games in Salt Lake City. But it was not just a matter of whether to continue skating at this level or not. For Michelle, now 17 years old, other things were happening as well. She was about to complete her high school studies and she had her eye on a number of different colleges, with Harvard topping the list. Despite being away from the classroom, Michelle had always been an excellent student and taken her studies very seriously. She spoke regularly with Karen, who was still studying at Boston University, and said she wondered what it would be like to have the kind of freedom most college students had.

But those thoughts would be put on hold, at least temporarily, as Michelle entered the most victorious stretch of her career. After Worlds, Michelle went on to win seven straight competitions through the rest of 1998, including the Goodwill Games. Later, this string of victories would help her put her loss at the Olympics in perspective. "A couple of hours of your life is not everything," she told a reporter. "You shouldn't let it determine whether you'll have success and happiness." That attitude seemed to stay with her through most of the year.

In August, after Michelle's 18th birthday, she did something that she had never done before: She took off a month from skating. The Kwans took a two-week vacation to Hawaii where Michelle went snorkeling and scuba diving, and when she came home she wanted to make other changes as well. She began by chopping off the shoulder-length hair she had always had into a short pixie cut. When she went to a pro-am competition in September and skated onto the ice after her name was announced, at first the crowd was quiet. "I don't think they recognized me," she said.

Any anonymity Kwan had did not last long. As the year wore on and she continued to rack up wins, Michelle kept one eye on the upcoming National and World championships. Then, in early 1999, Michelle continued her streak, scoring a victory over 13-year-old newcomer Naomi Nari Nam at Salt Lake City's Delta Center. This was Michelle's second consecutive U.S. Championship title and her third win in four years. But her roll ended soon after.

At the World Championships in Helsinki, Finland, in late March of 1999, Kwan was again the heavy favorite to take the gold medal. But after catching a cold, Michelle delivered mediocre performances in both the short and long program. She fell while attempting a double Axel in the short program and just grabbed the second spot in the long program. She managed to capture the silver medal, but just barely.

Giving It the Old College Try

That fall, Michelle enrolled part time at the University of California at Los Angeles. After winning back-to-back gold medals at Skate America and Skate Canada in the space of two weeks, she returned to Los Angeles to begin her new life as a college student. Her coach, Frank Carroll, once a student-athlete himself, said Michelle—who had worked with tutors since eighth grade—would have to learn how to divide her time now that she was attending classes. "At school, it's all school," Carroll said. "She can't be thinking about a double Axel when she's trying to nail a philosophy course. And the same thing with skating. She can't worry about an exam or what a professor said to her that she didn't like this morning when she's supposed to be out doing her long program."

School did not hinder Michelle's skating. As she readied herself for the 2000 U.S. and World Championships,

Kwan's winning streak continued. She took the gold medal in the 2000 Japan Open early in the year and a silver medal at the Grand Prix Finals. At Nationals in Cleveland, Ohio, more than 115,000 fans turned out over the course of the event. Michelle did not deliver her best performance—she fell in both her short and long programs—but she managed to come from behind to win the gold medal. With her 20th birthday less than five months away, Michelle took stock of the 14- and 15-year-old skaters she was competing against. "This was my seventh Nationals and I felt ancient next to these people," she said.

But she was not too old to win the World Championships in Nice, France, a month later. She was getting noticed outside the rink, too. A couple days before Nationals, Michelle signed a million-dollar deal with Chevrolet, and she was appearing in television specials for ABC as well. That year *People* magazine added Kwan to its list of 50 most beautiful people. She also had a video game, *Michelle Kwan Figure Skating*, designed after her.

Strained Relations

Michelle took some time off that summer, but when she returned to the ice that fall there seemed to be some cracks in her and longtime coach Frank Carroll's relationship. At the first event of the 2000–01 season—Skate America in Colorado Springs, Colorado—Kwan managed to take the gold medal, but her performance was not one of her best. She landed her opening jump two-footed and simplified one of her combinations. "It was a tough and cautious beginning of the program," she said afterward. "But as it progressed, I got a little stronger."

That did not seem to impress Carroll who, after Michelle's win, told his pupil she needed to show up for practice at their training facility in El Segundo, California, early the following Monday. "You know what he said to me?" Kwan told a reporter. "He said, 'So are you going to come at 8:30 Monday?' And he was dead serious."

Strains may have been showing between coach and student in late 1999 when Carroll said the following about Michelle's performance at Skate Canada in New Brunswick: "She has a lot of people telling her she is the greatest thing in the world, and I think it's good for her to stand back and listen to me about it and sometimes realize that she's not the greatest in the world and that there are areas she can improve on."

But with the new season under way, Michelle was poised to become one of the most winning figure skaters ever. She settled for silver medals in the next couple competitions, Skate Canada and the Canadian Open, but by then Nationals and Worlds were just around the corner.

At the 2001 U.S. National Championships in Boston in late January, Michelle skated in front of more than 15,000 fans. She did not disappoint them either, earning seven 6.0 scores for artistry in her short program. She was at her peak in her long program, as she pulled down two more perfect scores for artistry and seven 5.9s. The gold medal made Michelle the first woman since 1980 to win four national titles (Linda Fratianne won from 1977–80) and the first since Janet Lynn to win five in all (Lynn won hers from 1969–73). Despite the victory, Michelle admitted that winning "doesn't get easier. It gets harder and harder." Regardless, Kwan once again headed to Worlds.

Major Changes

Michelle had begun the year by making some changes in her appearance, program, and music. She told an interviewer that changing aspects of herself and her performances is a necessary challenge, even if she doesn't know how fans and judges are going to react. "Even if it's not as well liked as I hope, it's still a change and that's what matters," she said. "That you're growing and you're not staying the same."

She was about to face one of the biggest changes—and challenges—to her career that she had encountered. After winning the 2001 Worlds in Vancouver, Canada, at the start of the new season in the fall of 2001, Michelle decided to fire Frank Carroll. Earlier in the year Kwan, now 21 years old, had placed second in a few competitions. Carroll's dismissal, which came just days before Michelle's appearance at Skate America, resulted in rampant rumors and speculation as to what had happened. This talk increased when Kwan failed to name a new coach to replace Carroll. With the 2002 Winter Olympics barely six months away, the press and skating fans and critics could hardly believe that Michelle would attempt to train alone. But Michelle did her best to sidestep the rumors in the media. "People can write what they want, no matter what I say or feel," she said. "[But] I'm feeling a lot better on the ice, and that's all that matters to me."

As if to rebuff her critics, Michelle skated to first place at Skate America in October 2001. Although she led after the short program, Kwan was less than satisfied with her performance. But, she reasoned, "I've been through a lot of things in the last several weeks. Actually, the last several months." The rest of the year, she said, would be like a giant countdown until the Olympics.

The numbers seemed to skip a step just a week later at Skate Canada. For the first time since her 1996 performance at Centennial on Ice, Kwan finished in third place. Overall, it was her worst finish in seven years, since her 1995 World Championship performance at the age of 14. Michelle was in second place at the end of the short program, trailing 15-year-old skater Sarah Hughes. It was the second time Hughes had led Kwan in competition. But during the long program at Saskatchewan Place arena in Saskatoon, Canada, Kwan fell twice—once during her opening triple-toe/triple-toe combination.

"There are points when I'm worried, but there's one good thing I learned from this," she told reporters after her performance. "I'm gutsy. Even though I missed my first triple-triple, I tried the second one." But she also said that it might take a while for her to get her performance just right.

On Top of Nationals

Before long, however, Michelle began her climb back up. With the 2002 U.S. Championships less than a couple months away—and the Olympics right after—Michelle needed something to jump-start her skates. She got the momentum she needed at the Grand Prix Final in Kitchener, Canada, in mid-December, where she finished in second place behind Russia's Irina Slutskaya. This time, the silver medal was a victory for Michelle. Her main goal, she said after she had skated, was just to feel comfortable on the ice again. That feeling had been lacking from her performances for most of the year.

What exactly had changed for Michelle at the Grand Prix was not certain, but she seemed to have some of the hunger that had been missing from her routines. Whatever it was, as the New Year rolled around, she was back near her top form when she won the gold medal at the U.S. Figure Skating Championships in mid-January at Los Angeles's Staples Center in front of a hometown crowd of more than 18,000 fans. She nailed six triple jumps. While it wasn't Kwan's finest performance ever, it was the best fans had seen in a while. Before she even finished her program the crowd began its ovation.

The win put Michelle Kwan back on top of America's women skaters—and seemed to give her a renewed force for the 2002 Games, which were starting in less than a month. Four years had passed since Michelle had taken the silver medal to Tara Lipinski. Now she had won her sixth U.S. title, which put her ahead of skating legends such as Peggy Fleming and Janet Lynn. For years Michelle had told people that she wanted to be a skating legend. "I want people to remember me after 1,000 years," she said. Although 2001 had been a tough year, the past four years had been incredibly successful for Michelle. An Olympic gold medal would go a long way toward ensuring that her memory burned on.

6

KWAN SKATES ON

"No matter how good you are, the ice is still slippery," Danny Kwan had said this to his younger daughter many times. Michelle's biggest slip, and perhaps her most disappointing, would come at the 2002 Games in Salt Lake City. The figure skating world had expected a showdown between Michelle and Irina Slutskaya of Russia. Slutskaya had come on strong, besting Kwan in six competitions in two years. Michelle was considered the more graceful skater, but Irina, despite being one year older than her counterpart, was thought to be more daring and athletic. To add to the competition, 16-year-old Sarah Hughes and 17-year-old Sasha Cohen, a couple of promising young skaters, joined Michelle on the U.S. Olympic team.

As the Games edged closer, it became clear that Michelle would be going without a coach. She had managed a respectable first-place showing at Nationals, although her programs still allowed room for improvement. But going into the Olympics she told a reporter that winning the Games is an athlete's defining moment. "I don't believe you can ever truly be a legend without winning it," she said. She likened the skater's role to that of a gladiator's, "because, in the end, the toughest person usually wins."

But during the long program on February 21, 2002, toughness was not enough. In a surprising upset, Kwan took third place, behind gold-medal teammate Hughes and second-place winner Slutskaya. At the end of the competition, Michelle was a bit dumbfounded as to what had taken place. Like in Nagano four years before, she was upstaged by an American teenager. "Tonight it was one of those things. I don't know what didn't go my way." She landed a triple jump on two feet and fell during a triple flip. She had also skated without much of the fire that had marked her recent competitions. Michelle tried to put a good face on the experience, telling reporters, "I've experienced so much the last four years, and I realized it doesn't matter the color of your medal." But her tears reflected the disappointment she felt.

In March 2002, Michelle again finished behind Slutskaya at the World Championships. Although she failed to capture the gold, Kwan did land a triple-toe/triple-toe combination in the qualifying round—a move that had eluded her all year. It turned out to be a small victory, when she could not complete the maneuver during the final round against her Russian competitor.

Michelle gives it her all at the 2002 Winter Olympics in Salt Lake City, Utah. (Getty Images)

There was some consolation for Michelle after the Olympics and the World Championships. For one thing, she was receiving a lot of work from companies that wanted to use her image in their ads. Chevrolet, which already had a contract with her, extended its deal after the 2002 Games. A spokeswoman for the company said that the fact that Michelle did not win a gold medal didn't matter. "Her value to us doesn't decrease because she doesn't have a gold medal. The original reasons we liked Michelle hold up today."

Tom Collins, producer of the figure skating show Champions on Ice, echoed that sentiment. "I've been in skating 55 years and I've never seen anyone handle things so well, good or bad. A lot of it was bad at the two Olympics, but she accepted her defeat with graciousness," he said. After Worlds Michelle went on a five-month tour with Champions on Ice for 93 shows, earning a reported $1 million for her performances. But the big question after the 2001–02 season was whether or not Michelle was going to continue to compete. Would she try again for the gold medal in the 2006 Olympics at the ripe old age of 25?

"In the zone . . ."

Michelle took a much-needed break for most of the 2002–03 season, only entering one competitive event, Skate America, on short notice after Sarah Hughes dropped out because of an injury. Despite a mediocre performance (Michelle later called it "icky") she won the competition. Around the same time as her win, she hired Scott Williams, a former skating pro, choreographer, and longtime friend to help her. His role, Michelle later said, was not so much of a coach as it was a teammate. "I didn't need anyone [at that time] to really push me, because I felt like I just wanted to relax a little bit," she said.

Whatever her approach, it paid off. At her next competition, the 2003 National Championships in Dallas in January, Michelle skated to victory over her rival Sarah Hughes, winning her seventh national title, second only in the record books to Olympian Maribel Vinson Owen's nine titles, which were won between 1928 and 1937. More important, the win reaffirmed Michelle's decision to continue competing. "I was born July 7, and that's all I thought, that seven [titles] would be nice," she told reporters afterward.

But Michelle wasn't done—not by a long shot. Two months later at the World Championships in Washington, D.C., the 22-year-old skater offered a beautiful long program to capture her fifth world title. Skating to the music *Concierto de Aranjuez*, Kwan landed all seven of her planned triple jumps, seemingly with ease. "Athletes talk about being in the zone," she said afterward. "I feel like I'm walking through time, about to float on air."

One person in the stands had a banner that read "Kwan 2006 We Believe," and on this night thousands of other fans believed as well. Despite competing in just a few events during the 2002–03 season, Michelle deemed it a very relaxing year. "Maybe it tells me something: that I should put less pressure on myself, just go out there and have fun," she said. "I've had such a long, wonderful skating career. I think everything else is extra."

Looking Ahead

In the spring of 2003 Michelle was back at work with Champions on Ice, embarking on a 27-city tour that began in April. In the fall she competed in a couple of events, including the International Figure Skating Challenge in which she took first place. Then, late in the year, she made a move that indicated Michelle Kwan certainly has her eye on the future. On the advice of her choreographer, Michelle took her skates to Rafael Arutunian, a figure skating coach who is also adept at repairing equipment.

Arutunian adjusted her skates several times, and offered advice about what she could do to improve her technique. He had helped Michelle in the past with some of her jumps, and that is the kind of instruction she will need if she is going to participate in the 2006 Olympics. "If I look into the future for the Olympics, it's like, 'OK, if I want to do it, maybe Rafael can take me all the way,'" she said. After viewing tapes of her performances from the previous year, Michelle was convinced that she had been skating the same way for some time. "I think I need to step it up a notch," she added. "I have to keep on pushing myself and keep moving because the competition is becoming extreme, with triple-triples and triple Axels. I have to keep up with the times."

She seemed to do just that at the 2004 National Championships in Atlanta. Although she had a bit of a problem during her short program, Michelle came back from second place to edge out Sasha Cohen in the long program and win the national gold medal for the eighth time. However, she wasn't so successful at the World Championships in Dortmund, Germany, a couple months later, where she went home with the bronze.

But while she was there she seemed to be thinking more about what lay ahead for her than she was dwelling on the outcome of the event. After all, she had cruised to a victory at Nationals and this was her 11th appearance at Worlds. She was about to become an aunt—her sister Karen gave birth that spring—and she was still enrolled at UCLA, having declared her major in psychology.

At 23, she had dedicated the last 18 years of her life to skating, but there was one thing missing: an Olympic gold medal. Just two years separated her from the 2006 Olympic Games in Turin, Italy, and this trip overseas

Michelle's family has always been her main source of support and encouragement. She is seen here on the left with her mother, Estella, and her sister, Karen. (Getty Images)

seemed to call that possibility to mind more than anything else. "I thought that after 2002 I would finish competing, but the reason I'm here is because I love it," she told reporters. "I have one more shot for Turin now. It's my destiny."

TIME LINE

1980 Born in Torrance, California, July 7

1985 Begins skating at the age of 5

1986 Starts taking private skating lessons

1988 Wins first junior competition

1991 Goes to Ice Castle International Training Center in Lake Arrowhead, California, with sister, Karen

1992 Passes test to skate at senior ladies level

1993 Wins Regionals and Sectionals on way to her first Nationals event; wins women's singles at Olympic Festival

1994 Wins silver medal at first Nationals; serves as an alternate at Olympics, but does not compete; places eighth in first Worlds

1995 Places second in Nationals and fourth in Worlds

1996 Wins U.S. and World Figure Skating Championships
at the age of 15

1997 Takes the silver medal in National and World
Championships

1998 Wins U.S. and World Championships en route to
Olympics, but takes the silver medal to Tara
Lipinski's gold at the Olympics

1999 Wins gold at Nationals and silver in Worlds; enrolls
at UCLA

2000 Wins gold in National and World Championships

2001 Wins gold in National and World Championships;
fires coach Frank Carroll

2002 Wins gold at Nationals and silver in Worlds; takes
bronze medal in 2002 Winter Games in Salt Lake City

2003 Wins gold in National and World Championships;
hires new coach Rafael Arutunian

2004 Wins gold at eighth Nationals; takes bronze in
Worlds; says she will continue to skate until
2006 Olympics

HOW TO BECOME A PROFESSIONAL ATHLETE

THE JOB

Professional athletes participate in individual sports such as tennis, figure-skating, golf, running, or boxing, competing against others to win prizes and money.

Depending on the nature of the specific sport, most athletes compete against a field of individuals. The field of competitors can be as small as one (tennis, boxing) or as large as the number of qualified competitors, anywhere from six to 30 (figure skating, golf, cycling). In certain individual events, such as the marathon or triathlon, the field may seem excessively large—often tens of thousands of runners compete in the New York Marathon—but for the professional runners competing in the race, only a handful of other runners represent real competition.

The athletic performances of those in individual sports are evaluated according to the nature and rules of each specific sport. For example, the winner of a foot race is whoever crosses the finish line first; in tennis the winner is the one who scores the highest in a set number of games; in boxing and figure skating, the winners are determined by a panel of judges. Competitions are organized by local, regional, national, and international organizations and associations whose primary functions are to promote the sport and sponsor competitive events. Within a professional sport there are usually different levels of competition based on age, ability, and gender. There are often different designations and events within one sport. Tennis, for example, consists of doubles and singles, while track and field contains many different events, from field events such as the javelin and shot put, to track events such as the 110-meter dash and the two-mile relay race.

Athletes train year-round, on their own or with a coach, friend, parent, or trainer. In addition to stretching and exercising the specific muscles used in any given sport, athletes concentrate on developing excellent eating and sleeping habits that will help them remain in top condition throughout the year. Although certain sports have a particular season, most professional athletes train rigorously all year, varying the type and duration of their workouts to develop strength, cardiovascular ability, flexibility, endurance, speed, and quickness, as well as to focus on technique and control. Often, an athlete's training focuses less on the overall game or program that the athlete will execute, than on specific areas or details of that game or program. Figure skaters, for example, won't simply keep going through their entire long programs from start to finish but instead will focus on the jumps, turns, and hand movements that refine the program. Similarly, sprinters don't keep running only the sprint distances they race in during a meet; instead, they vary their workouts to include some distance work, some sprints, a lot of weight training to build strength, and maybe some mental exercises to build control and focus while in the starter's blocks. Tennis players routinely spend hours just practicing their forehand, down-the-line shots.

Athletes often watch videotapes or films of their previous practices or competitions to see where they can improve their performance. They also study what the other competitors are doing in order to prepare strategies for winning.

REQUIREMENTS

High School

A high school diploma will provide you with the basic skills that you will need in your long climb to becoming a professional athlete. Business and mathematics classes will teach you how to manage money wisely. Speech classes will help you become a better communicator. Physical education classes will help you build your strength, agility, and competitive spirit. You should, of course, participate in every organized sport that your school offers and that interests you.

Some individual sports such as tennis and gymnastics have professional competitors who are high school students. Teenagers in this situation often have private coaches with whom they practice both before and after going to school, and others are home-schooled as they travel to competitions.

Postsecondary Training

There are no formal education requirements for sports, although certain competitions and training opportunities are only available to those enrolled in four-year colleges and universities. Collegiate-level competitions are where most athletes in this area hone their skills; they may also compete in international or national competitions outside of college, but the chance to train and receive an education isn't one many serious athletes refuse. In fact, outstanding ability in athletics is the way many students pay for their college educations. Given the chances of striking it rich financially, an education (especially a free one) is a wise investment and one fully supported by most professional sports organizations.

Other Requirements

There is so much competition to be among the world's elite athletes in any given sport that talent alone isn't the primary requirement. Diligence, perseverance, hard work, ambition, and courage are all essential qualities to the individual who dreams of making a career as a professional athlete. "If you want to be a pro, there's no halfway. There's no three-quarters way," says Eric Roller, a former professional tennis player who competed primarily on the Florida circuit. Other, specific requirements will vary according to the sport. Jockeys, for example, are usually petite men and women.

EXPLORING

If you are interested in pursuing a career in professional sports you should start participating in that sport as much and as early as possible. With some sports, an individual who is 15 may already be too old to realistically begin pursuing a professional career. By playing the sport and by talking to coaches, trainers, and athletes in the field, you can ascertain whether you like the sport enough to make it a career, determine if you have enough talent, and gain new insight into the field. You can also contact professional organizations and associations for information on how to best prepare for a career in their sport. Sometimes there are specialized training programs available, and the best way to find out is to get in contact with the people whose job it is to promote the sport.

EMPLOYERS

Professional athletes who compete in individual sports are not employed in the same manner as most workers. They do not work for employers, but choose the competitions or tournaments they wish to compete in. For example, a professional runner may choose to enter the Boston Marathon and then travel to Atlanta for the Peachtree Road Race.

STARTING OUT

Professional athletes must meet the requirements established by the organizing bodies of their respective sport. Sometimes this means meeting a physical requirement, such as age, height, or weight; and sometimes this means fulfilling a number of required stunts, or participating in a certain number of competitions.

Professional organizations usually arrange it so that athletes can build up their skills and level of play by participating in lower-level competitions. College sports, as mentioned earlier, are an excellent way to improve one's skills while pursuing an education.

ADVANCEMENT

Professional athletes advance into the elite numbers of their sport by working and practicing hard, and by winning. Professional athletes usually obtain representation by sports agents in the behind-the-scenes deals that determine which teams they will be playing for and what they will be paid. These agents may also be involved with other key decisions involving commercial endorsements, personal income taxes, and financial investments of the athlete's revenues.

A college education can prepare all athletes for the day when their bodies can no longer compete at the top level, whether because of age or an unforeseen injury. Every athlete should be prepared to move into another career, related to the world of sports or not.

EARNINGS

The U.S. Department of Labor reports that athletes had median annual earnings of $45,780 in 2003. Ten percent earned less than $13,310.

Salaries, prize monies, and commercial endorsements will vary from sport to sport; a lot depends on the popularity of the sport and its ability to attract spectators, or on the sport's professional organization and its ability to drum up sponsors for competitions and prize money. Still other sports, like boxing, depend on the skill of the fight's promoters to create interest in the fight. An elite professional tennis player who wins Wimbledon, for example, usually earns more than half a million dollars in a matter of several hours. Add to that the incredible sums a Wimbledon champion can make in endorsements and the tennis star can earn more than one million dollars a year. This scenario is misleading, however; to begin with, top athletes usually cannot perform at such a level for very long, which is why a good accountant and investment counselor comes in handy. Secondly, for every top athlete who earns millions of dollars in a year, there are hundreds of professional athletes who earn less than $40,000. The stakes are incredibly high and the competition fierce.

Perhaps the only caveat to the financial success of an elite athlete is the individual's character or personality. An athlete with a bad temper or prone to unsportsmanlike behavior may still be able to set records or win games, but he or she won't necessarily be able to cash in on commercial endorsements. Advertisers are notoriously fickle about the spokespeople they choose to endorse products;

some athletes have lost million-dollar accounts because of their bad behavior on and off the field of play.

Other options exist, thankfully, for professional athletes. Many go into some area of coaching, sports administration, management, or broadcasting. The professional athlete's unique insight and perspective can be a real asset in careers in these areas. Other athletes have been simultaneously pursuing other interests, some completely unrelated to their sport, such as education, business, social welfare, or the arts. Many continue to stay involved with the sport they have loved since childhood, coaching young children or volunteering with local school teams.

WORK ENVIRONMENT

Athletes compete in many different conditions, according to the setting of the sport (indoors or outdoors) and the rules of the organizing or governing bodies. Track-and-field athletes often compete in hot or rainy conditions, but at any point, organizing officials can call off the meet, or postpone competition until better weather. Indoor events are less subject to cancellation. However, since it is in the best interests of an organization not to risk the athletes' health, any condition that might adversely affect the outcome of a competition is usually reason enough to cancel or postpone it. An athlete, on the other hand, may withdraw from competition if he or she is injured or ill. Nerves and fear are not good reasons to default on a competition and part of ascending into the ranks of professional athletes means learning to cope with the anxiety that competition brings. Some athletes actually thrive on the nervous tension.

In order to reach the elite level of any sport, athletes must begin their careers early. Most professional athletes have been working at their sports since they were small children; skiers, figure skaters, and gymnasts, for example, begin skiing, skating, and tumbling as young as age two or three. Athletes have to fit hours of practice time into an already full day, usually several hours before school, and several hours after school. To make the situation more difficult, competitions and facilities for practice are often far from the young athlete's home, which means they either commute to and from practice and competitions with a parent, or they live with a coach or trainer for most of the year. Separation from a child's parents and family is an especially hard and frustrating element of the training program. When a child has demonstrated uncommon excellence in a sport, the family often decides to move to the city in which the sports facility is located, so that the child doesn't have to travel or be separated from a normal family environment.

The expenses of a sport can be overwhelming, as can the time an athlete must devote to practice and travel to and from competitions. In addition to specialized equipment and clothing, the athlete must pay for a coach, travel expenses, competition fees and, depending on the sport, time at the facility or gym where he or she practices. Tennis, golf, figure skating, and skiing are among the most expensive sports to enter.

Even with the years of hard work, practice, and financial sacrifice that most athletes and their families must endure, there is no guarantee that an athlete will achieve the rarest of the rare in the sports world—financial reward. An athlcte needs to truly love the sport at which he or she excels, and also have a nearly insatiable ambition and work ethic.

OUTLOOK

The outlook for professional athletes will vary depending on the sport, its popularity, and the number of athletes currently competing. On the whole, the outlook for the field of professional sports is healthy, but the number of jobs will not increase dramatically. Some sports, however, may experience an increase in popularity, which will translate into greater opportunities for higher salaries, prize monies, and commercial endorsements.

TO LEARN MORE ABOUT PROFESSIONAL ATHLETES

BOOKS

Boitano, Brian, and Suzanne Harper. *Boitano's Edge: Inside the Real World of Figure Skating.* New York: Simon & Schuster, 1997.

Christopher, Matt. *On the Ice with Tara Lipinski.* Matt Christopher Sports Biographies. New York: Little, Brown, 1999.

Morrissete, Mike. *Nancy Kerrigan: Heart of a Champion.* Sports Illustrated for Kids Books. New York: Bantam, 1994.

Petkevitch, John Misha. *Figure Skating: Championship Techniques.* Sports Illustrated Winners Circle Books. New York: Sports Illustrated Books, 1989.

Yamaguchi, Kristi, Christi Ness, and Jodi Meacham. *Figure Skating For Dummies.* Hoboken, N.J.: John Wiley and Sons, 1997.

ORGANIZATIONS AND WEBSITES

Individuals interested in becoming professional athletes should contact the professional organizations for the sport in which they would like to compete, such as the National Tennis Association, the Professional Golf Association, or the National Bowling Association. Ask for information on requirements, training centers, and coaches. The following organization may also be able to provide further information:

American Alliance for Health, Physical Education, Recreation, and Dance

1900 Association Drive

Reston, VA 20191-1598

Tel: 800-213-7193

http://www.aahperd.org

For a free brochure and information on the Junior Olympics and more, contact

Amateur Athletic Union

PO Box 22409

Lake Buena Vista, FL 32830

Tel: 407-934-7200

http://www.aausports.org

TO LEARN MORE ABOUT MICHELLE KWAN AND FIGURE SKATING

BOOKS

Brennan, Christine. *Inside Edge*. New York: Doubleday, 1996.

———. *Edge of Glory*. New York: Simon & Schuster, 1998.

Epstein, Edward Z. *Born to Skate: The Michelle Kwan Story*. New York: Ballantine Books, 1997. *

Kwan, Michelle. *Heart of a Champion*. New York: Scholastic Inc., 1997. *

————. *The Winning Attitude! What It Takes to Be a Champion* (as told to Laura James). New York: Hyperion Books, 1999. *

*Young adult books

MAGAZINES AND NEWSPAPERS

Carnes, Jim. "Kwan Is Not Ready to Skate into Sunset," *Sacramento Bee*, 23 April 2004, metro, 16.

Clarey, Christopher. "Kwan Wins Her Fifth World Title; Cohen Finishes Fourth," *The New York Times*, 30 March 2003, sports, 1.

Elliott, Helene. "Kwan Does Just Enough," *Los Angeles Times*, 29 October 2000, sports, 5.

————. "First Part of Kwan's Solo Act Is Successful," *Los Angeles Times*, 26 October 2001, sports, 3.

————. "Verdict Goes to Kwan," *Los Angeles Times*, 28 October 2001, sports, 1.

————. "Favorites Get Caught Short," *Los Angeles Times*, 3 November 2001, sports, 7.

————. "Hughes Is Golden as Kwan Slips," *Los Angeles Times*, 4 November 2001, sports, 11.

————. "Kwan Cuts Through All of Coaching Speculation," *Los Angeles Times*, 13 November 2001, sports, 1.

————. "Second Place Makes Kwan Comfortable," *Los Angeles Times*, 16 December 2001, sports, 1.

————. "Good as Gold," *Los Angeles Times*, 17 September 2002, sports, 1.

————. "Injured Yagudin Has His Eye on the Cash," *Los Angeles Times*, 13 December 2002, sports, 9.

————. "Kwan Is in Seventh Heaven," *Los Angeles Times*, 19 January 2003, sports, 1.

————. "Kwan Is Still Living in Her Magical Moment," *Los Angeles Times*, 4 April 2003, sports, 18.

Hersh, Philip. "New Coach Helps Energize Kwan," *Chicago Tribune*, 25 December 2003, sports, 1.

Jones, Todd. "Figure Skating on Thin Ice as Any Sort of Sport," *The Columbus Dispatch*, 14 February 2000, 1C.

Neill, Mike. "High Hopes," *People* 51, no. 11 (March 29, 1999): 85.

Park, Alice. "Amazing Grace," *Time* 151, no. 5 (February 9, 1998): 85–89.

————. "Spin City," *Time* 159, no. 6 (February 11, 2002): 44–47.

————. "Leap of Faith," *Time* 159, no. 9 (March 4, 2002): 56–58.

Penner, Mike. "Judge Flips Over Kwan's Program," *Los Angeles Times*, 9 January 1998, sports, 1.

————. "Victorious Kwan Close to Perfection," *Los Angeles Times*, 11 January 1998, sports, 1.

———. "Blithe Lipinski Flies to Gold in Figure Skating," *Los Angeles Times*, 21 February 1998, news, 1.

Powers, John. "Four More Years," *Boston Globe*, 21 January 2001, D1.

Rosewater, Amy. "Record Crowd Impresses Group," *The Plain Dealer*, 14 February 2000, 14D.

Smolowe, Jill. "Fire on Ice," *People* 57, no. 3 (January 28, 2002): 124–126, 128.

Starr, Mark. "Iron Will, Golden Dreams," *Newsweek* 129 (February 17, 1997): 52–54.

———. "Flying on Ice," *Newsweek* 131 (February 9, 1998): 58–62.

———. "Kwan Song," *Newsweek* 139, no. 7 (February 18, 2002): 50–55.

Swift, E.M. "A Star Is Reborn," *Sports Illustrated* 88, no. 2 (January 19, 1998): 49–50.

———. "Into the Light," *Sports Illustrated* 88, no. 5 (February 9, 1998): 114–118.

———. "She's Got Next," *Sports Illustrated* 90, no. 8 (February 22, 1999): 68, 70.

———. "Fall Guys," *Sports Illustrated* 94, no. 4 (January 29, 2001): 80–83.

———. "She's Gotta Have It," *Sports Illustrated* 96, no. 5 (February 4, 2002): 128–133.

Tresniowski, Alex. "Belle on the Ball," *People* 48, no. 20 (February 23, 1998): 213–214.

————. "Triple Threat," *People* 49, no. 7 (February 23, 1998): 94–100.

Wire reports. "Kwan Takes Skating Title," *Los Angeles Times*, 27 October 2002, sports, 17.

ORGANIZATIONS AND WEBSITES

"Cool on the Ice," CNN.com. Available online. URL: http://www.cnn.com/Programs/people/shows/kwan/profile.html. Downloaded on August 6, 2004.

"Sweet Sixteen," SI.com (Sports Illustrated). Available online. URL: http://sportsillustrated.cnn.com/olympics/2002/figure_skating/news/2002/02/21/womens_final_ap/. Posted on February 21, 2002.

"It's a Bummer," SI.com (Sports Illustrated). Available online. URL: http://sportsillustrated.cnn.com/olympics/2002/figure_skating/news/2002/02/21/kwan_future_ap/. Posted on February 22, 2002.

Stevens, Neil. "Michelle Kwan's Juggling Act a Success So Far," Slam Skating (Canadian Press). Available online. URL: http://www.canoe.ca/SkateCanada/nov7_mic.html. Posted on November 7, 1999.

Zanca, Salvatore. "Kwan, Weiss Make World Skating Hard to Figure," Slam Skating (Associated Press). Available online. URL:http://www.canoe.ca/SlamSkating99Worlds/mar28_wor.html. Posted on March 28, 1999.

U.S. Figure Skating Headquarters

20 First Street

Colorado Springs, CO 80906

Tel. (719) 635-5200

http://www.usfsa.org

Golden Skate

http://www.goldenskate.com

Skate Canada

865 Shefford Road

Ottawa, Ontario

K1J 1H9

Tel: (613) 747-1007

http://www.skatecanada.ca

International Figure Skating Online

http://www.ifsmagazine.com/glg

INDEX

Page numbers in *italics* indicate illustrations.

ABOUT THE AUTHOR

Freelance journalist and editor **Todd Peterson** spent several years writing about music and pop culture in northern California before moving to Las Vegas to cover southern Nevada's exciting entertainment scene. Todd moved to New York in 2001 where he continues to write about a variety of topics and edit other writers' work. He is the author of the Ferguson Career Biography *Tony Hawk: Skateboarder and Businessman.*

When he is not writing or editing, Todd is probably devouring a book or hiding out at the movies. He resides in Brooklyn with his wife and son.